The
EWT
Coach

MATHEMATICS

by Mervine Edwards

EDUCATIONAL DESIGN, INC.   EDI 212

TABLE OF CONTENTS

INTRODUCTION

This book will help you prepare for the New Jersey Early Warning Test in mathematics. It shows you what the questions on the test are like, and it tells you what you need to know to do well on the test. Finally, *The EWT Coach* will give you practice in using what you have learned.

There are 3 types of questions on the EWT Test:

• **Multiple-choice questions,** in which you pick the correct answer from a list of 4 choices. Most of the questions are of this kind.

• **Questions in which you write your answer** instead of picking it out from a list of choices.

• **Open-ended questions** (also called constructed-response questions), in which you both give your answer and write an explanation of how you got it.

Here are some tips to help you do well:

• **Answer all questions.** You can't get a question right if you don't answer it.

• **If a question is giving you lots of trouble, skip it.** Go on to the next question. Then. when you're through, go back and work on the questions you skipped.

• **Eliminate wrong answers.** If you aren't sure of the right answer to a multiple-choice question, try to get the correct answer by eliminating the wrong ones.

• **Guess if you have to.** It doesn't cost you anything to guess. And your guess may be correct, especially if you have eliminated one or two wrong answers.

• **Pay special attention to open-ended (constructed response) questions.** An open-ended question counts more than a multiple-choice question. You won't do well on the test if you do very badly on the open-ended questions. The next chapter in this book tells you how to answer this kind of question. Read it carefully.

Good luck on the test!

ANSWERING OPEN-ENDED QUESTIONS

Most of the questions on the EWT exam are multiple-choice questions. But there are a whole group of very important questions that are not. They are introduced by directions like these:

DIRECTIONS FOR QUESTIONS 17-18: Write your answers on page 5 in your answer folder. For each question, give enough explanation so that the scorer can understand your solution and write your response in the appropriate space. You will be graded on the quality of your thinking, as reflected in your explanations, as well as on the correctness of your responses.

Questions with directions like these are called *open-ended questions* or *constructed response questions*.

To answer an open-ended question, you have to do two things:

1. **Work out an answer to the question and write it down.**

2. **Write a good description of how you got your answer. That is, write directions that someone else could follow to get the correct answer.**

Just writing the correct answer isn't enough. You won't get full credit unless you give a good explanation of how you got the answer.

Writing a good explanation, even if you worked out the math wrong, gives you more credit than writing a correct answer with no explanation or with an explanation that a scorer cannot understand.

You get the most credit if you get the answer right and have a good explanation of how you got it.

An open-ended question may have two parts. For example, you might be asked to find the <u>area</u> and <u>perimeter</u> of an irregular geometric figure. In that case, you must write two answers and two explanations to get full credit for the question.

On the next page is an example of an open-ended question. You'll see it again in Lesson 14 of the book, so don't worry if you can't answer it now. The important thing is for you to notice how clear the answer is.

If the pattern of pennies shown in the three figures below is continued, how many pennies will be in the seventh group of pennies?

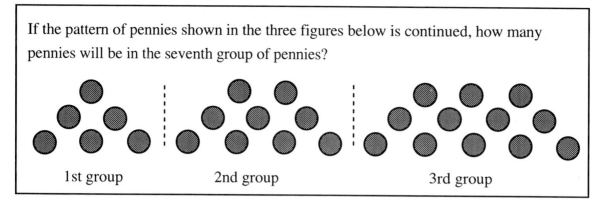

1st group   2nd group   3rd group

Here's one way you might answer an open-ended question like this one.

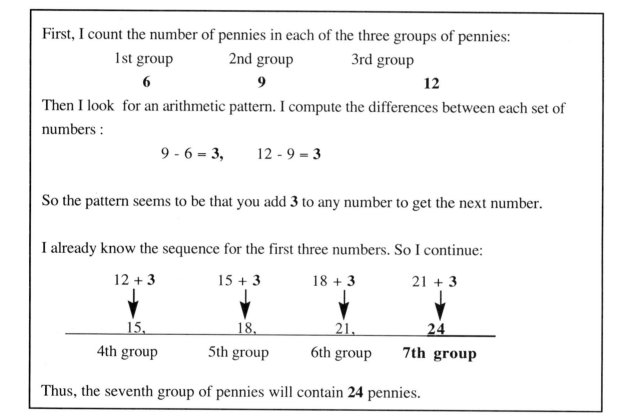

First, I count the number of pennies in each of the three groups of pennies:

1st group	2nd group	3rd group
6	**9**	**12**

Then I look for an arithmetic pattern. I compute the differences between each set of numbers :

$$9 - 6 = 3, \qquad 12 - 9 = 3$$

So the pattern seems to be that you add **3** to any number to get the next number.

I already know the sequence for the first three numbers. So I continue:

12 + **3**	15 + **3**	18 + **3**	21 + **3**
↓	↓	↓	↓
15,	18,	21,	**24**
4th group	5th group	6th group	**7th group**

Thus, the seventh group of pennies will contain **24** pennies.

There are more than 100 examples of how to answer different kinds of EWT questions in this book. Each example contains sections labeled **Strategy** and **Solution**. Study these sections. They do more than tell you how to do the examples. They also show you the kind of writing—and thinking—you must do to answer an open-ended question. When you come to the open-ended question in the Practice Tests at the end of each chapter, use the **Strategy** and **Solution** sections of the examples as models for your answers.

LESSON 1 NUMERICAL OPERATIONS
Choosing the Correct Operation

You can make it easier to solve word problems.
Learn to recognize from key words or phrases what operation of arithmetic to use.

Choosing whether to add or subtract

Certain key words and phrases indicate whether to add or subtract.

Phrases that tell you to add

Find the **total**
How much **altogether**

Example: Find the total of $40, $30, and $20.

$40 + $30 + $20 = $90   *Answer:* $90

Find the **sum**

Example: Find the sum of 4, 6, 7, and 8.

4 + 6 + 7 + 8 = 25   *Answer:* 25

Find 4 more than a number

Example: Find 4 more than 8.

8 + 4 = 12   *Answer:* 12

Phrases that tell you to subtract

Many word problems ask you to compare two numbers using the phrases below.

How much **less than**

Example: 2 is how much less than 6?

6 - 2 = 4   *Answer:* 4

Find the **increase** or **gain**

Example: Last week's basketball score was 55.
This week's score was 65. What was the increase?

65 - 55 = 10   *Answer:* 10

Find the **decrease, loss,** or **difference**

Example: Jon weighed 140 lb last week. This week his weight is 135 lb. How many pounds did he lose?

140 - 135 = 5   *Answer:* 5 pounds

How much more than

Example: 8 is how much more than 3?

8 - 3 = 5   *Answer:* 5

-1-

Notice the slight difference in the two uses of the phrase *more than* on the previous page.

How much more than one number is another?   **Find 4 more than** a number.

7 is how much more than 3?   Find 3 more than 7.

$$7 - 3 = 4$$ $$7 + 3 = 10$$

Answer: 4   Answer: 10

EXAMPLE 1   Find 7 more than 5.   9 is how much more than 6?

Strategy   This means **increase** 5 by 7.   This means **find the difference** between
                                                                9 and 6.

                    Add: $5 + 7 = 12$ Subtract: $9 - 6 = 3$

Solution   12   3

Frequently you will be asked to compare numbers presented in a **data table.**

Data tables will be studied in greater detail in a later lesson. However, you will be introduced to them below.

EXAMPLE 2   Use this table to answer the question below.

Amusement Park	Number of Female Employees	Number of Male Employees	Attendance (in millions)
Rides Galore	443	502	2.6
Happy Valley	952	723	1.9
True Fantasy	535	545	2.2
Fast Wheelers	384	461	1.0

According to this table, the number of female employees at Fast Wheelers was how much less than the number of male employees at Happy Valley?

Strategy   First use the table to find the number of:

   female employees at Fast Wheelers and

   male employees at Happy Valley.

(continued on next page)

**Strategy
(continued)**

Amusement Park	Number of **Female** Employees	Number of **Male** Employees	Attendance (in millions)
Rides Galore	443	502	2.6
Happy Valley	952	**723**	1.9
True Fantasy	535	545	2.2
Fast Wheelers	**384**	461	1.0

	384 females at **Fast Wheelers**	**723 males** at **Happy Valley**
Now **COMPARE**:	384 females	723 males

How much less than: Subtract.

$$\begin{array}{r} 723 \\ -\ 384 \\ \hline 339 \end{array}$$

Solution   So, there are **339** less females than males.

Sometimes it is helpful to use a calculator for your computations. This is illustrated below.

EXAMPLE 3   Use the table of Example 2 to find the total number of male employees at all the parks. Use a calculator for your calculation.

Strategy   " Find the **total** " tells you to **add.**
Add the numbers in the **Number of Male Employees column** .

Amusement Park	Number of Female Employees	**Number of Male Employees**	Attendance (in millions)
Rides Galore	443	**502**	2.6
Happy Valley	952	**723**	1.9
True Fantasy	535	**545**	2.2
Fast Wheelers	384	**461**	1.0

502 + 723 + 545 + 461
= 2,231

Enter 502, enter +, enter 723, enter +, enter 545, enter +, enter 461, enter =, READ 2231

Solution   Thus, the total number of male employees at all the parks is 2,231.

The ability to estimate answers is important, particularly when you are using a calculator. If you press the wrong key on a calculator, you may get an answer which is way off. Therefore, you need to be able to estimate the answer in advance so that you can determine if your calculator answer is reasonable. Most estimations are based upon **rounding.** Frequently, rounding to the **leftmost** place will usually give you a reasonable estimate for computations involving large whole numbers.

Rounding to the Leftmost Place

To round to the leftmost place:
1. If the 2nd digit in the numeral is 5 or more, increase the 1st digit by 1.   **(Round UP.)**
2. If the 2nd digit in the numeral is less than 5, leave the 1st digit unchanged. **(Round DOWN.)**

EXAMPLE 4   Round **3,951 and 739** to the leftmost place.

Strategy   3,951   **3** is the **leftmost** place.   739   **7** is the **leftmost** place.

3, **9** 5 1   7 **3** 9

↓   ↓

more than 5   less than 5

Therefore, **increase** 3 by 1.   Therefore, leave the **7 unchanged.**

Solution   Round 3,951 **up** to   Round 739 **down** to

4,000.   700.

This idea of rounding for estimation can now be used to determine if the result of Example 3 of the previous page is **reasonable.**

EXAMPLE 5   Use estimation to determine if the calculator answer, 2,231, is a reasonable answer for the sum 502 + 723 + 545 + 461.

Strategy   Round each of the added numbers to the leftmost place.

502 rounds to **500**	Add the rounded numbers: **500**
723 rounds to **700**	**700**
545 rounds to **500**	**500**
461 rounds to **500**	+ **500**
	2,200

Solution   The calculator result, **2,231**, rounds to **2,000**, which is reasonably close to **2,200.**

EXAMPLE 6   Using the standard procedure for rounding (**If the digit in the hundreds place is 5 or more, round up. Otherwise, round down.**), a township clerk rounds the population of a city to the nearest **thousand** and records it as 50,000. What is the greatest possible value for the actual population?

(A)   50,500   (B)   50,499

(C)   49,999   (D)   49,500

Strategy   Round each choice to the **nearest thousand.**

For the first choice, 50,500, note that the thousands and hundreds digits are:

50, 500

thousands   **hundreds**
digit   digit

50,**5**00	rounds to 51,000	Hundreds digit is **5** or more. Round **up.**
50,**4**99	rounds to 50,000	Hundreds digit is <u>less than 5</u>. Round **down.**
49,**9**99	rounds to 50,000	Hundreds digit is <u>more than 5</u>. Round **up.**
49,**5**00	rounds to 50,000	Hundreds digit is **5** or more. Round **up.**

Only the last three choices round to 50,000.

The greatest of these three, 50,499, 49,999, and 49,500 is **50,499.**

Solution   So, the solution is (B), 50,499.

EXAMPLE 7   According to a recent almanac, New York City was the most densely populated city in the U.S.A. There were 4,003,360 more people living in New York City than in Los Angeles, the second most densely populated city in the U.S.A. Los Angeles had a population density of 6,996 people per square mile. If the population of Los Angeles was 3,259,340, what was the population of New York City?

Strategy   First identify the numbers mentioned in the problem. Which are needed?

4,003,360 more people in N.Y.C. than in Los Angeles

6.996 population density of Los Angeles

3,259,340 population in Los Angeles

Only the first and the third relate to what you are asked to find, **population.**

You are **not** interested in the population **density**, 6,996.

-5-

Strategy (continued)   Now use these two relevant numbers to find the population of N.Y.C.

N.Y.C. population 4,003,360 more than Los Angles population 3,259,340

4,003,360 <u>more than</u> 3,259,340

    Add: **4,003,360 + 3,259,340**

7,262,700

Solution   Thus, the population of N.Y.C must be **7,262,700** according to the almanac.

SUMMARY

In Questions 1-5, indicate whether you must add or subtract.

1.   7 is how much more than 2?
2.   Find 9 more than 6.
3.   5 is how much less than 12?
4.   Find the sum of 8 and 19.
5.   Last week's earning were $75. This week's earnings were $95.
      Find the increase.

How do you round each of the following to the leftmost place?

6.   4,752   7. 829

8.   How can you determine if the calculator answer for $401 + 893 = 745 + 219$
      is reasonable ?

9.   Use the table of Example 2, page 2, to answer the question below.
      How can you find how many more male employees were at True Fantasy than at
      Rides Galore?

SAMPLE EWT QUESTIONS

1.   Find 23 more than 39.
      A. 6   B. 16   C. 52   D. 62

2.   How much more than 59 is 73?
      A. 6   B. 14   C. 122   D. 132

3. Find the total of the week's sales of televisions: 4 on Monday, 7 on Tuesday, 5 on Wednesday, 7 on Thursday, and 6 on Friday.
   A. 24   B. 29   C. 32   D. 40

4. Last Wednesday, the girls basketball team scored 65 points. This Monday, they scored 56 points. Find the decrease in this week's score.
   A. 9   B. 19   C. 111   D. 121

Use this table to answer the questions below.

Enrollment in Eighth Grade Math Courses at Smartzee Junior High School		
Course	Girls	Boys
EWT Prep	25	15
Math Survey	55	60
Algebra	45	51
Algebra Honors	19	17

5. How many more girls are in Algebra than in EWT Prep?
   A. 5   B. 6   C. 10   D. 20

6. How many less boys are in EWT Prep than in Algebra Honors?
   A. 2   B. 32   C. 36   D. 45

7. How many students altogether are in Math Survey?
   A. 40   B. 96   C. 115   D. 134

8. The number of students in EWT Prep is how much less than the number of students in Math Survey?
   A. 30   B. 45   C. 65   D. 75

9. Find the total number of girls in all math courses.
   A. 143   B. 134   C. 144   D. 287

10. Find the sum of the numbers of all math students.
    A. 115   B. 144   C. 287   D. 300

11. The total number of girls is how much more than the total number of boys?
    A. 1   B. 2   C. 5   D. 10

The EWT also contains questions which are not multiple choice. Exercises 12-18 are examples of questions like this. For each one, solve the problem and write the answer.

On the actual test you will be asked to use a grid on which you write your response. So these types of exercises are referred to as **grid response exercises**.

 Use your calculator to answer Exercises 12–13, then check to make sure your answers are reasonable by rounding to the leftmost place,

12. Tanya's earning for five months at a part-time job were $49, $112, $79, $42, and $197. Find her total earnings for the five months.

13. The population of Little Stone is 49,978. The population of Big Rock is 60,119. How much greater is the population of Big Rock than the population of Little Stone?

14. Round each price to the nearest dollar and estimate the subtotal of the prices of the receipt. The subtotal of the prices is between _____.
    (A) $7 and $9
    (B) $11 and $13
    (C) $15 and $17
    (D) $19 and $21

```
COUNTRY MARKET          KEY
$ 2.16  MT              GTX- General
$ 1.04  PR                   Taxable Item
$ 0.88  GR              GR-  Grocery
$ 2.43  MT              MT-  Meat
$ 0.25  PR              Pr-  Produce
$ 1.10  GTX            SUB- Subtotal
$ 0.68  GTX
$ 5.11  MT
$ 0.72  PR
$ 1.35  GTX
SUB $
TAX
TOTAL $
```

15. Nazir works after school at a part-time job. He works 3 hours on Monday, 4 hours on Wednesday, and 2 hours on Friday. His pay for the three days is $15 on Monday, $20 on Wednesday, and $10 on Friday. How much does he earn altogether for the week?

16. Sonya bought seven items indicated on the receipt at the right. If she gave the clerk a twenty-dollar bill and a penny to pay for her purchases, how much change should the clerk give her?

```
Jersey Shore Grocery
$6.43
$2.99
$2.92
$0.79
$1.95
$0.83
$1.05
_____  TOTAL
```

17. The city of Gainsville had a school budget of $11,498,785 last year. 25,456 of the 32,563 voters voted against this year's school budget of $12,045,339. This year's budget represented an increase of how much over last year's budget?

Most of the questions on the EWT exam are either multiple-choice or grid-response questions. But there is a whole group of very important questions that are neither. They are introduced by directions like the ones below.

Questions with directions like these are called **open-ended questions** or **constructed-response questions.** Strategies for answering such questions will be explained throughout this text.

OPEN-ENDED QUESTIONS

DIRECTIONS FOR QUESTION 18-19: Write your answer to the following question. Also give enough explanation so that anyone reading your solution can understand your method. On the EWT you will be graded on the quality of your thinking, as reflected in your explanation, as well as the correctness of your response.

18. Use the table of Example 2, page 2, to answer the following question:
Which is larger, the total number of male employees or the total number of female employees?
The smaller total is how much less than the larger total?

19. Renee has an appointment to see her doctor exactly three weeks from today. Today is April 16th. On what date is her appointment with the doctor?

APRIL						
Sun	Mon	Tues	Wed	Thur	Fri	Sat
			1	2	3	4
5	6	7	8	9	10	11
12	13	14	15	16	17	18
19	20	21	22	23	24	25
26	27	28	29	30		

LESSON 2   NUMERICAL OPERATIONS
Choosing the Correct Operation, Part 2

In the last lesson you reviewed key phrases that told you whether to **add** or **subtract**.
The following example will suggest a pattern for determining whether **multiplication** or **division** is the key to the solution of a word problem.

EXAMPLE 1   Solve the following word problems.

There are 14 books in a carton. How many books are in **17** cartons?	5 tapes cost $35.95. Find the cost of **1** tape.

Strategy

How many in **several?**

↓

MULTIPLY

$14 \times 17 = 238$

Find the cost of **one.**

↓

DIVIDE

$35.95 \div 5 = 7.19$

Solution   Thus, there are 238 books.

Thus, each tape costs $7.19

This suggests the following for determining whether to multiply or divide.

> To find how many of **several**, **MULTIPLY.**
> To find how many of **each** or **one**, **DIVIDE.**

In business it is common practice to **always** round a cost **UP**. Thus if a clerk uses a calculator to divide, the clerk will round **up** to the next higher penny if the division is not exact.

EXAMPLE 2   Carla is shopping for magic markers and wants the lowest price per marker.
Which choice below will give her what she wants?
   A. 1 dozen for $4.88
   B. 2 dozen for $9.30
   C. 4 for $1.62
   D. 3 for $1.21

(continued on next page)

Strategy   Finding the cost **per** marker is the same as finding the cost of **each**.

For each choice, **DIVIDE**. Select the **least** result.

A. 1 dozen = 12: $4.88 \div 12 = 0.466666$ Round **UP** to 0.47

B. 2 dozen = 2 · 12 = 24: $9.30 \div 24 = 0.3875$ Round **UP** to 0.39

C. $1.62 \div 4 = 0.405$ Round **UP** to 0.41

D. $1.21 \div 3 = 0.4033333$ Still round **UP** to 0.41

The least result is 0.39.

Solution   Thus, the best choice is B.

Recall that multiplication can be indicated by a raised dot.

Thus, 30 x 40 can be written as 30 · 40.

EXAMPLE 3   Mr. Sorkowitz ordered exactly 30 calculators for each of the 40 classrooms in the junior high school where he was principal. In response to that order, a total of 1,225 calculators was delivered to his school. Based on this information, which statement below is true?

A. The correct number of calculators was delivered.

B. The school needed 25 more calculators.

C. Not enough calculators were delivered.

D. Too many calculators were delivered.

Strategy   Find the total number he ordered, using 30 calculators for each of 40 rooms.

To find how many of several, multiply.

30 · 40 = 1,200.

More than 1,200 were delivered.

Therefore, too many were delivered.

Solution   The correct choice is D.

Sometimes the EWT contains a sample advertisement that gives much more information than you need to solve a problem.

You have to look at only the data in the advertisement that the problem discusses.

This is illustrated in the next example.

EXAMPLE 4 Use the information in this advertisement to answer the question below.

The Gazette News				
Mail Subscription Rates				
	1 mo.	3 mos.	6 mos.	1 year
Weekdays and Sundays	$17.35	$50.25	$97.50	$185.00
Weekdays	$12.45	$36.95	$72.00	$141.00
Sundays	$4.45	$12.85	$26.25	$48.00
Home Delivery Rates by Carrier				
Weekdays and Sundays	$2.35/week			
Weekdays	$1.60/week			
Sundays	$0.85/week			
Weekends (Fri., Sat., & Sun)	$1.35/week			

About how much would be saved by ordering a one-year mail subscription to the *Gazette News* for weekdays and Sundays at the special one-year subscription rate, compared to the monthly rate for that same type of subscription?

Strategy   There are two sets of rates: Mail Subscription Rate

Home Delivery Rate by Carrier

But you don't need the Home Delivery Rate to answer the question..

You are only asked about: **Mail Subscription Rate for Weekdays and Sundays**

Comparing monthly rate with yearly rate

	Mail Subscription Rates			
	1 mo.	3 mos.	6 mos.	**1 year**
Weekdays and Sundays	**$17.35**	$50.25	$97.50	**$185.00**
Weekdays	$12.45	$36.95	$72.00	$141.00
Sundays	$4.45	$12.85	$26.25	$48.00

1. Find the cost for a year using the monthly rate of $17.35 for 12 months.
    To find the cost of several, multiply: $17.35 · 12 = **$208.20**

2. The savings is the monthly rate for a year minus the yearly rate.

        $208.20   -   **$185**   = $23.20

Solution   Thus, the savings is $23.20.

EXAMPLE 5   A custodian is setting up chairs in the gym for an eighth grade class meeting. He is setting up 219 chairs, all in rows of exactly 17 chairs, except for the last row. How many chairs are in the last row?

Strategy   To find how many of each or one you divide.

Find $219 \div 17$.

Using a calculator, you get an answer of 12.882353: 12 rows with .882353 row left over. We want the number of chairs in that last row.

Multiply: 0.882353 times 17 = 15   Without the computer:
(rounded)

$$\begin{array}{r} \underline{12} \text{ seats per row} \\ 17\,)\,219 \\ \underline{17} \\ 49 \\ \underline{34} \\ 15 \text{ seats in the last row} \end{array}$$

Solution   Thus there will be **15** seats in the last row.   **15** seats in the last row

Suppose that your test grades for 4 tests are 80, 100, 96, and 100. How do you find your average for the four tests?

Step 1   Add the four scores: $80 + 100 + 96 + 100 = 376$

Step 2   Divide the sum by the number of tests, 4: $376 \div 4$ or $\dfrac{376}{4} = 94$

Thus the **average** or the **mean** for the four tests is 94.

DEFINITION: Average

To find the average for a set of numbers (values):

1.   Add all the values.

2.   Divide the sum by the n, the total number of values.

$$\text{Average} = \frac{\text{sum of the numbers}}{n}$$

An **average** is also called a **mean**.

EXAMPLE 6 Meg's test scores are 95, 80, 95, 80, and 95. Find her mean score for the five tests.

Strategy Add the scores for the five tests .

Enter 95, enter +, enter 80, enter +, enter 95, enter +, enter 80, enter +, enter 95, enter =,

Solution Divide the result by 5. Thus, the mean is 89.

enter ÷ , enter 5, enter =. Read 89.

A faster way of doing the addition in Example 6 above involves using the **Order of Operations rule**.

Order of Operations

When several operations occur,

1. compute all multiplications and divisions first in order from left to right,

2. then compute all additions and subtractions in order from left to right.

Thus, to find the sum of the five test scores 95, 80, 95, 80, and 95,

think: (3 · 95)   +   (2 · 80)

              ↓   ↓

              285   +   160   **Multiply first.**
                    445   **Add.**

Doing this by calculator is illustrated below.

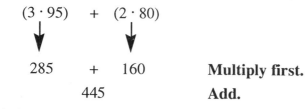

                    3 · 95   +   2 · 80

Enter 3, enter **x**, enter 95, enter +, enter 2, enter **x**, enter 80, enter =
Read 445. (Warning: This will not work on certain kinds of calculators.)

We now connect ideas from both this lesson and the last lesson.

The next example involves finding the average of a set of numbers in a data table like the ones you studied in Lesson 1.

EXAMPLE 7   Find the mean of the populations of the four cities in the table below.

City	Altitude (feet)	Population (1986)	Area (square miles)
Boston	10	573,000	47.2
Chicago	623	3,009,500	228.1
Houston	49	1,728,910	572.7
Newark	146	316,240	24.1

Strategy   Find the average of the 4 numbers in the Population column.

City	Altitude (feet)	**Population (1986)**	Area (square miles)
Boston	10	**573,000**	47.2
Chicago	623	**3,009,500**	228.1
Houston	49	**1,728,910**	572.7
Newark	146	**316,240**	24.1

Enter 573000, enter +, enter 3009500, enter +, enter 1728910,

enter +, 316240, enter =

enter ÷, enter 4, enter =

Read 1406912.5

Solution   Thus, the average of the 4 populations is 1,406,912.5

We close this lesson with a technique for drawing conclusions from a data table or a chart like the one of Example 7 above.

EXAMPLE 8   Use the table of Example 7 above to find the city with the following characteristics.

- The city has a population of more than 400,000.
- Its altitude is below 50 feet.
- Its area is less than 300 square miles.

(continued on next page)

Strategy

1. In the **Population** column, put an asterisk next to the three numbers more than 400,000.

City	Altitude (feet)	**Population (1986)**		Area (square miles)
Boston	10	**573,000**	*	47.2
Chicago	623	**3,009,500**	*	228.1
Houston	49	**1,728,910**	*	572.7
Newark	146	316,240		24.1

2. In the **Altitude** column, put an asterisk next to the two numbers less than 50.

City	**Altitude (feet)**		Population (1986)		Area (square miles)
Boston	**10**	*	573,000	*	47.2
Chicago	623		3,009,500	*	228.1
Houston	**49**	*	1,728,910	*	572.7
Newark	146		316,240		24.1

3. In the **Area** column, put an asterisk next to the three numbers less than 300.

City	Altitude (feet)		Population (1986)		**Area (square miles)**	
Boston	10	*	573,000	*	**47.2**	*
Chicago	623		3,009,500	*	**228.1**	*
Houston	49	*	1,728,910	*	572.7	
Newark	146		16,240		**24.1**	*

4. Look for the **City** row that has **3 asterisks**.

City	Altitude (feet)		Population (1986)	Area (square miles)	
3 asterisks **Boston**	**10**	*	**573,000** *	**47.2**	*
Chicago	623		3,009,500 *	228.1	*
Houston	49	*	1,728,910 *	572.7	
Newark	146		316,240	24.1	*

Solution

Thus, Boston is the only city that has all three characteristics.

SUMMARY

1.   If you know the cost of one item, how do you find the cost of several?

2.   A school bus can transport at most 40 students. How do you find the least number of busses to transport 205 students to an away-football game?

3.   Use the table from Example 4, page 12, to answer this question.

     The Jamisons want the *Gazette* by mail subscription on weekdays and Sundays.

     How do you find the amount saved by using the year rate instead of the one-month rate?

4.   How do you find the average of 5 numbers?

5.   What other word is frequently used to indicate the **average** of a set of numbers?

6.   Use the table of Example 7 to answer the question below.

     How do you find the city with the following characteristics?

     •   The city has a population of more than 600,000?

     •   Its altitude is less than 50 feet.

     •   Its area is greater than 50 square miles.

SAMPLE EWT QUESTIONS

1.   A six-pack of soda cans costs $4.50. Find the cost of 1 can of soda.
     A. $0.75   B. $27.00   C. $4.56   D. $0.80

2.   A carton of yearbooks contains 28 yearbooks. How many books are contained in 7 cartons?
     A. 4   B. 21   C. 196   D. 206

3.   Which of the following is the best buy for pens?
     A. 1 dozen for $10.80   B. 2 dozen for $20.40
     C. 3 for $2.85   D. 4 for $3.73

4.   Mr. Angster ordered 30 new desks for each of the 35 classrooms in the junior high where he is principal. The desk company shipped 950 desks. Which statement below is true?
     A. Too many desks were delivered.   B. 100 desks had to be sent back.
     C. There were just enough desks.   D. Not enough desks were delivered.

Use the table from Example 4 to answer Exercises 5-7 below.

5. How much would Sunday home delivery cost for a year?

    A. $3.40   B. $10.20   C. $44.20   D. $45.00

6. How much would be saved by ordering a one-year subscription for Sundays compared to the monthly rate for the same type of subscription?

    A. $5.40   B. $6.40   C. $43.55   D. $53.40

7. How much would be saved by ordering a one-year subscription for weekdays compared to the six-months rate for the same type of subscription?

    A. $69   B. $21.75   C. $3.00   D. $2.50

8. An assembly-line worker is packaging textbooks in cartons for shipment of an order of 87 books to a school. If each carton holds at most 9 books, how many books will be in the last carton?

    A. 5   B. 6   C. 9   D. 783

9. Tina's bowling scores for 5 games were 225, 180, 180, 225, and 180. Find her mean score for the 5 games.

    A. 110   B. 118   C. 190   D. 198

10. Using the table of Example 7, find the mean altitude for the four cities.

    A. 207   B. 206.775   C. 179.95   D. 182

11. Abdul is packing boxes ot cassette tapes. He packs 7 tapes per box. Since he began, he has packed 103 cassette tapes. Which box is he now packing?

    A. 5 th   B. 13th   C. 14 th   D. 15 th

12. A waiter earns an average of $54.00 each day from tips left by customers. If he works from 6 to 8 hours per day, about how much money per hour does he earn, on average, from tips?

    A. $4.00 to $5.50   B. $6.75 to $8.00

    C. $6.75 to $9.00   D. $9.00 to $11.00

13. Eighty years ago, a man, age 71, walked from Jersey City to Los Angeles, a distance of approximately 3,000 miles. It took him 105 days to complete the walk. How many miles per day, on average, did he walk?

   A. 70 miles   B. 41 miles   C. 30 miles   D. 4 miles

Use this table to answer Exercises 14-17.

Car	Cost (basic model)	Length	Weight
Grand Marquis	$22,130	212.4 inches	3,784 lb
Sable	$17,460	192.2 inches	3,119 lb
Tracer	$10,155	170.9 inches	2,344 lb
Villager	$17,015	189.9 inches	3,768 lb

14. Find the average cost of these four types of Mercury automobiles.

15. Find the mean weight for the four models.

16. Identify the model with the following characteristics.
   - length more than 190 inches
   - costs more than $11,000
   - weight less than 3,200 lb

17. Identify the model with the following characteristics.
   - costs less than $18,000
   - length less than 190 in
   - weighs more than 2,200 lb but less than 3,200 lb

18. A store sells soda at a rate of six cans for $3.19. A customer wants only one can. The clerk divides $3.19 by 6 using his calculator to find the price. The calculator displays 0.531666666. Assuming that the store requires rounding up to the nearest cent, what should the clerk charge the customer?

19. A stationery store sells ball-point pens at a rate of a dozen pens for $5.90 and boxes of notepaper at a rate of three boxes for $8.60. Assume that the store requires rounding up to the nearest cent. Find the total cost , without sales tax, for one pen and one box of notepaper.

20. Use this advertisement to answer the question below.
What is the least amount it would cost to buy the parts to build a skateboard—one board, two trucks, and four wheels?

SPECIAL SKATEBOARD SALE	
Trucks (axles)	$35-$45 each
Boards	$55-$80 each
Each pair of wheels	$15-$25 each

OPEN-ENDED QUESTION

21. The graduating eighth grade wants to rent a banquet room for their prom.
They must pay $300 to rent the hall plus $25 per person for dinner.
Explain your answer to each question below.

    A.   Which expense will not change no matter how many people come to the prom?

    B.   Suppose that at least 50 but not more than 90 people are expected to come to the prom. What are the least and greatest amounts of money that the prom could cost?

REVIEW

1. So far, Tanya has saved $130 for a pair of rollerblades and all of the safety equipment listed at the right. Which of the following is the closest estimate of what she needs to save to buy all of these things?
Tanya needs about:
A. $10 more   B. $30 more
C. $40 more   D. $70 more

Roller Blades Special at the Sports King Store	
Rollerblades	$68.96
Helmet	$29.25
Knee Pads	$20.05
Elbow Pads	$15.99
Wrist Guards	$26.15

2. Which of these decimals is closest to the product (multiplication) of 0.54 and 0.0019?
    A. 0.01   B. 0.001   C. 0.0001   D. 0.00001

3. Find 19 more than 38.
    A. 9   B. 19   C. 47   D. 57

4. How much more than 19 is 50?
    A. 69   B. 41   C. 31   D. 21

Use this chart to answer Exercises 5-6.

5. Which of these statements can be supported using the chart?

    A. Females need fewer calories at age 11 than at age 8.

    B. As they get older, the energy needs of females increase.

    C. As they get older, the energy needs of females decrease.

    D. As they get older, the energy needs of females increase and then decrease.

DAILY ENERGY NEEDS FOR FEMALES	
Age	Calories
3	1,350
6	1,900
11	2,500
21	2,000
60	1,500

6. The number of calories needed at age 60 is how much less than that needed at age 6?

    A. 150   B. 400   C. ,850   D. 3,400

7. Leroy bought four items indicated on the receipt. If he gave the clerk a ten-dollar bill and two pennies to pay for his purchases, how much change should the clerk give him?

RECEIPT: Garden Produce
$1.95
$2.73
$1.18
$3.11
_____ TOTAL

 Use rounding to the leftmost place to check for reasonableness of your answers by calculator.

8. Ms. Hendricks' purchases of Fall clothes were $39, $101, $89, $78, and $101. Find her total expenses at the department store.

9. Jonas bought 5 pounds of roast beef for a party at $8.99 a pound.
    He pays the bill with two twenties and a ten.
    Find the change the clerk should give him.

LESSON 3   NUMERICAL OPERATIONS
Fractional Part of a Number

This drawing shows 7 squares. 3 of the 7 squares are shaded.

This idea can also be expressed as a fraction:

$\frac{3}{7}$ of the squares are shaded.

Notice that **4** out of the **7** squares are not shaded.

$\frac{4}{7}$ of the squares are **not** shaded.

This suggests a pattern, as shown in the example below.

EXAMPLE 1   A team wins $\frac{5}{9}$ of the games it plays.

What fractional part of the games are lost if there are no ties?

Strategy   Think:

$\frac{5}{9}$ won means **5** out of 9 <u>won</u>. So the number <u>lost</u> must be 9 - 5, or **4** .

4 out of 9 **lost.**

Solution $\frac{4}{9}$ is the fractional part of the games lost.

An important application of the ideas above involves finding a fractional part of a number.

To find $\frac{2}{3}$ of a number, you can use several different methods.

First, recall that in mathematics, *of* means **"times"** or **"multiply."**

So, $\boxed{\frac{2}{3} \textbf{ of } 12}$ means $\boxed{\frac{2}{3} \cdot 12}$.

$\frac{2}{3} \cdot 12$ can be done by **3** methods.

Method 1	**Method 2**	**Method 3**
$\frac{2}{3} \cdot 12 = \frac{2}{\cancel{3}} \cdot \cancel{12}^{4} = \textbf{8}$	$2 \cdot 12 = 24$	$12 \div 3 = 4$
	$24 \div 3 = 8$	$2 \cdot 4 = \textbf{8}$

EXAMPLE 2 The field hockey team of Jonas Junior High won $\frac{3}{4}$ of the 16 games it played this season. How many games were lost?

Here are two ways to solve this problem.

Strategy

Method 1

1. Find the number won.

   Find $\frac{3}{4}$ of 16

   $$\frac{3}{\underset{1}{\cancel{4}}} \cdot \overset{4}{\cancel{16}} = 12$$

2. Find the losses:

   games played - games won = losses

   $$16 \quad - \quad 12 \quad = 4$$

Thus, the team lost **4** games.

Method 2

1. $\frac{3}{4}$ won means

   3 out of 4 won

   So,   1 out of 4 were lost.

   $\frac{1}{4}$ of games were lost.

2. Find $\frac{1}{4}$ of 16 or $\frac{1}{4} \cdot 16$

   $$\frac{1}{\underset{1}{\cancel{4}}} \cdot \overset{4}{\cancel{16}} = 4$$

Thus, the team lost **4** games.

Solution The result is the same by both methods.
4 games were lost.

EXAMPLE 3 Pam ran exactly 20 times around a quarter-mile track.
How many miles did she run?

Strategy one-quarter $= \frac{1}{4}$

$$20 \cdot \frac{1}{4} \qquad \textbf{To find several if you know one, you multiply.}$$

$$\overset{5}{\cancel{20}} \cdot \frac{1}{\underset{1}{\cancel{4}}} = 5$$

Solution Thus, the run was 5 miles.

The next application of multiplying by a fraction involves the idea of time.

There are 60 minutes in an hour.

So, if something happens every 20 minutes, it will happen **3** times in an hour (**60 ÷ 20 = 3**).

EXAMPLE 4   Every 20 minutes, the number of bacteria in a science experiment approximately doubles.

The population at 4 P.M. was about one quarter of a million bacteria.

Find the approximate size of the population at 6 P.M.

Strategy   "Population doubles" means **multiply** population by **2**.

From 4 p.m. to 6 p.m. there are **2 hours.**

There are 60 minutes to 1 hour.

There are **3** 20-minute intervals in every **60** minutes or **1 hour.**

So there are **6** 20-minute intervals in **2** hours.

So, the population doubles **6** times in **2** hours.

The starting population is one-quarter million, or $\frac{1}{4}$ million.

Multiplying the population by 2 every 20 minutes for **6** intervals is

$\frac{1}{4}$ million · $\boxed{2 \cdot 2 \cdot 2 \cdot 2 \cdot 2 \cdot 2}$. This is **NOT** the same as multiplying by 12.

Think: $\frac{1}{4}$ · $\boxed{64}$

$$\frac{1}{\underset{1}{\cancel{4}}} \cdot \overset{16}{\cancel{64}} = 16$$

Solution   Thus, the approximate size of the population at 6 P.M. is 16 million.

Frequently, stores offer customers a **discount** to encourage them to buy.

If a store advertises a $20 discount on a radio that regularly sells for $100, the customer pays $100 - $20, or $80.

This idea can be expressed as a formula.

Regular Price -   Discount = Sale Price
$100   - $20   = $80

Stores advertise **discounts** two ways:

(1)   in terms of percent **(taught in the next lesson)**

(2)   in terms of a fractional part **off** the regular price

Discount in terms of a fractional part off the regular price is illustrated in the next example.

EXAMPLE 5 A football is advertised at a special discount of $\frac{1}{3}$ off the regular price of $52. Find the sale price rounded to the nearest cent.

Strategy Find $\frac{1}{3}$ **of** 52

$$\frac{1}{3} \cdot 52$$

$$\frac{1}{3} \cdot \frac{52}{1} = \frac{52}{3} \qquad \frac{52}{3} \text{ means } 52 \div 3.$$

$$= 17.333333 \qquad \textbf{3 does not divide 52 exactly.}$$

The discount rounds to $17.33   17.33**3**333 **3 is less than 5. Round down.**

Find the sale price.

Regular Price -   Discount   = Sale Price
    $52   - $17.33   = $34.67

Solution Thus, the sale price is $34.67, rounded to the nearest cent.

The work for solving Example 5 can be shortened for calculator use as indicated below. First, recall the rule for **Order of Operations:**

When an expression has several operations, do multiplications and divisions first, then additions and subtractions.

Think: Sale Price = Regular Price - Regular Price ÷ 3.

Enter 52   enter -   enter 52   enter ÷   enter 3   enter =
Read 34.66667   Round to 34.67
Thus, the sale price is $34.67, the same result as in Example 4.

EXAMPLE 6 José and Tina have a coupon that will allow them to buy a hot dog at half price if they buy one at full price. At full price, the hot dog costs $1.80. If they use the coupon, which method below could be used to find the total cost of the two hot dogs?

A. Divide $1.80 by 2, then subtract that amount from $1.80.

B. Multiply $1.80 by 2, then subtract half that amount from $1.80.

C. Multiply $1.80 by one-half, then subtract that amount from $1.80.

D. Divide $1.80 by 2, then add that amount to $1.80.

(continued on next page)

-25-

Strategy   First find the cost of a hot dog at half price. This can be done two ways:

1. Multiply $1.80 by $\frac{1}{2}$ or

2. Divide $1.80 by 2.

Now find the cost of the two by adding this result to $1.80, the cost of one.

Solution   This is the same as Choice D.

SUMMARY

1. If a team wins $\frac{4}{7}$ of the games it plays, how do you find the fractional part of the games lost?

2. How do you find a fractional part of a number?

3. What are three ways to find $\frac{4}{5}$ of 15?

4. The girls basketball team won $\frac{2}{3}$ of the 12 games they played. What are two ways to find the number of games lost?

5. Gina ran 14 times around a half-mile track. How do you find the number of miles she ran?

6. Start with the number 8. This number is doubled after 10 minutes. The new number is doubled after another 10 minutes. If this doubling is continued every 10 minutes for a half-hour, how do you find the final result?

7. What is a discount?

8. A camera is advertised at a discount of $\frac{1}{4}$ off the regular price of $61. How do you find the sale price rounded to the nearest cent?

9. A coupon allows you to buy a tape at $\frac{1}{3}$ off the regular price if you buy one at the full price of $9. How do you find the cost of buying two tapes using this coupon?

SAMPLE EWT QUESTIONS

1. What fractional part of all the squares are shaded?

2. What fractional part of all the squares are not shaded?

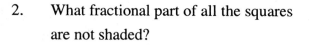

3. A football team lost $\frac{3}{5}$ of the 15 games played this season. How many games were won if there were no ties?

   A. 9   B. 6   C. 5   D. 3

4. Roscoe, a star baseball player, gets a hit about $\frac{1}{3}$ of the time. If he batted 636 times, what should be his approximate total of hitless at-bats?

   A. 424   B. 414   C. 318   D. 212

5. Tony ran exactly 32 times around a quarter-mile track. How many miles did he run?

   A. 8   B. 9   C. 24   D. $32\frac{1}{4}$

6. Wanda swam three-eighths of a mile 16 times this month. How many miles did she swim?

   A. 2   B. 5   C. 6   D. 10

7. Monica has a large collection of cassette tapes. Jane has half as many tapes as Monica. Which of these statements contains the same information?

   A. Monica has half as many tapes as Jane.

   B. Jane has twice as many tapes as Monica.

   C. Monica has twice as many tapes as Jane.

   D. Jane has as many tapes as Monica.

8. Paul and Doreen have a coupon that lets them buy one chicken dinner at half-price if they buy one full-price dinner at Kansas Fried Chicken. A full-price meal costs $5.35. If they use the coupon, find the total cost for the two dinners.

   A. $2.67   B. $2   C. $8.02   D. $8.03

9. An advertisement states: **"Buy one roll of 135 mm film at the regular price of $3.95, get a second roll at half-price."**

   Which of these methods could be used to find the total cost of two rolls of film?

   A. Divide $3.95 by 2, then add the amount to $3.95

   B. Multiply $3.95 by 2, then subtract half that amount from $3.95.

   C. Divide $3.95 by 2, then subtract that amount from $3.95.

   D. Multiply $3.95 by one-half, then subtract that amount from $3.95.

10. Which of the following is a way to find $\frac{4}{5}$ of a number?

    A. Multiply the number by $\frac{5}{4}$.

    B. Multiply the number by 4, then divide the result by 5.

    C. Divide the number by 4, then multiply the result by 5.

    D. Divide the number by 4, then divide the result by 5.

11. A radio is advertised at a special discount of $\frac{1}{3}$ off of the regular price of $73. Find the sale price rounded to the nearest cent.

    A. $24.33   B. $24.34   C. $48.66   D. $48.67

12.   I Every year we spend $5 million on exercise programs and $20 million on hot dogs.

    II Every year, we spend $\frac{1}{5}$ as much on exercise programs as we do on hot dogs.

    III Every year, we spend $\frac{1}{4}$ as much on exercise programs as we do on hot dogs.

    Which statements above are equivalent to each other?

    A. I and II only   B. I and III only

    C. II and III only   D. I, II, and III

13. As part of a biology experiment, Tasha is growing bacteria from left-over food. Every 20 minutes, the number of bacteria in the population approximately doubles. The population at 10:00 A.M. was about half a million bacteria. Which of these most likely represents the size of the population at noon?

    A. more than 30 million   B. between 4 and 8 million

    C. about 4 million   D. between 10 and 20 million

14. Every fifteen minutes, the number of bacteria in a science experiment approximately doubles. The population at 5 P.M. was about one quarter of a million bacteria. Find the approximate size of the population at 6 P.M.

15. Find the sale price of a catcher's mitt that is discounted at $\frac{1}{5}$ off of its regular $45 price.

16. The number 12 is increased by $\frac{1}{4}$ of itself. What is the new number?

17. An eighth-grade field hockey team played 20 games this season. Two games were tied. The team won $\frac{3}{4}$ of the games played. How many games did the team lose?

OPEN-ENDED QUESTIONS

18. A football team played 15 games this season. Three games were tied. The team lost $\frac{1}{3}$ of the games played. How many games were won? Explain in detail how you got your answer.

19. Ajax Records advertises $\frac{1}{4}$ off the regular $8.00 price of its new cassette tapes. Musac Enterprises advertises: "Buy a tape at the regular $8.00 price and get a second tape at half-price." Which is the better buy? Prove by actual numerical results that your answer is correct.

REVIEW

1. A consumer report for young people rated seven brands of book packs and found the following results:

A. Brand S
B. B and U
C. Brand Y
D. Brand W

Book Pack Brand	Price	Durability Scale: 5-highest 1-lowest	Comfort Scale: 5-highest 1-lowest	Total Score
R	$55	3	3	6
S	$38	4	1	5
T	$24	2	3	5
U	$16	4	3	7
V	$23	1	2	3
W	$41	4	3	7

Which brand is the most durable for the least price?

2. A carton contains 12 books. How many books are contained in 6 cartons?
   A. 2   B. 18   C. 60   D. 72

3. Which is the best buy for cans of soda?
   A. 2 dozen for $7.20   B. 4 for $1.25
   C. 3 for $1.05   D. $3.00 for a dozen

4. Find the mean score for the following bowling scores: 180, 250, 140, 200, and 300.

5. Of 954 kids recently surveyed, about half of them receive a weekly allowance plus extra money each week. Based on this and the table below, which of the following statements is true on the average?

Age Range	Weekly Allowance	Total Weekly Money
10-and 11-year-olds	$4.00	$7.00
12-and 13-year-olds	$5.00	$11.00
14-and 15-year-olds	$9.00	$18.00

A. Each week, 10- and 11-year-olds get more as extra money than their allowance.

B. Each week, 12- and 13-year-olds get more as extra money than their allowance.

C. Each week, 14- and 15-year-olds get twice as much extra money as their allowance.

D. Each week, 14- and 15-year-olds get more as extra money than their allowance.

6. How much more than 29 is 50?
    A. 79   B. 39   C. 31   D. 21

7. Find 19 more than 70.
    A. 41   B. 51   C. 61   D. 89

8. Which of these decimals is closest to the product of 0.46 and 0.0039?
    A. 0.00002   B. 0.0002   C. 0.002   D. 0.02

9. Jack has an appointment for a job interview exactly two weeks from today. Today is April 22. On what date is his interview?

APRIL						
Sun	Mon	Tues	Wed	Thur	Fri	Sat
			1	2	3	4
5	6	7	8	9	10	11
12	13	14	15	16	17	18
19	20	21	22	23	24	25
26	27	28	29	30		

10. A store sells manila envelopes at the rate of a dozen for $6.74 and pens at 3 for $1.00. Assume that the store requires rounding up to the nearest cent. Find the total cost, without sales tax, for one pen and two envelopes.

LESSON 4   NUMERICAL OPERATIONS
Percent of a Number

Percent means **hundredths**.

75% means $\frac{75}{100}$, or 0.75   Think in terms of money: 75 cents

4% means $\frac{4}{100}$, or 0.04   Think in terms of money: 4 cents

150% means $\frac{150}{100}$, or 1.50   Think in terms of money: 150 cents

In the last lesson you learned how to find a fractional part of a number.

For example, to find $\frac{1}{5}$ **of** 35, you multiply $\frac{1}{5}$ times 35.

Thus, $\frac{1}{5}$ of 35 means $\frac{1}{5} \cdot 35$.

$\frac{1}{5}$ can also be written as a decimal.

$$\frac{1}{5} = 0.20$$

$$\begin{array}{r} 0.20 \\ 5\overline{)1.00} \end{array}$$

So, $\frac{1}{5}$ **of** 35 can be thought of as

> **0.20 of** 35 or
>
> **20 hundredths of** 35 or
>
> **20% of** 35 (**Remember, percent means hundredths.**)

So,   20% of 35 means 0.20 **of** 35

      20% of 35 means $0.20 \cdot 35$

This suggests that to find a percent of a number, you change the percent to a decimal and then multiply the number by this decimal.

Therefore,

      30% of 40 means **0.30 · 40**   **30% = 0. 30**

      3% of 40 means **0.03 · 40**   **3% = 0. 03**

      125% of 40 means **1.25 · 40**   **125% = 1. 25**

EXAMPLE 1   Find the total cost of a $350 stereo, including a 6% sales tax.

Strategy 1   There are two ways to find the total cost.

METHOD 1:

Step 1   Find the tax: 0.06 · $350 = $21.00

Step 2   **Then find the total cost.**

Solution 1   **$350 + $21.00 = $371.00.**

Strategy 2   **METHOD 2:**

THINK: A 6% sales tax means you pay an additional $.06 on every dollar.

So, you are paying $1.00 + $.06, or **$1.06** on every dollar that the stereo costs.

Now, you can find the total; cost in **one step.**
Multiply: 350 · 1.06 = $371.00

Solution 2   The result is the same as in **Method 1: $371.00.**

EXAMPLE 2   A skirt that regularly sells for $25 is on sale at a discount of 30%. Which of the procedures below could you use to find the sale price?

   I   25 - (0.30)(25)   II   (25)(0.30)
   III   (25)(1.30)   IV   (25)(0.70)
   (A)   I only   (B)   I or IV only
   (C)   IV only   (D)   II or III only

There are two ways to find the sale price.
METHOD 1:

Strategy   Step 1   Multiply $25 by 0.30 to find the **discount.**

Step 2   Subtract the **discount** from $25:   25 - **discount.**

This method is described by **Choice I** above: **25 - (0.30) (25).**

A second method is illustrated on the next page.

METHOD 2:

THINK :   a 30% **discount** means $0.30 **saved** on every dollar.

Thus, you pay **$1.00 - $.30** or

↓

$.70 on every dollar

Now, you can find the sale price in one step. **Multiply $25 by 0.70.**

This is illustrated in **Choice IV** on the previous page: (25)(0.70)

Thus, the procedure for finding the sale price is **I or IV**.

Solution   So, **(B)** is the correct multiple-choice response.

EXAMPLE 3   Teresa usually makes 70% of her basketball foul shots.

This season she attempted 163 foul shots.

Approximately how many foul shots did she miss this season?

Strategy   70% of the shots **made** means she **made** 70 out of 100 shots.

Therefore, she **missed 30 out of 100** shots.

↓

So, she **missed**   **30%**   of the shots.

Find   30%   of   163.

0.30   ·   163

48.9

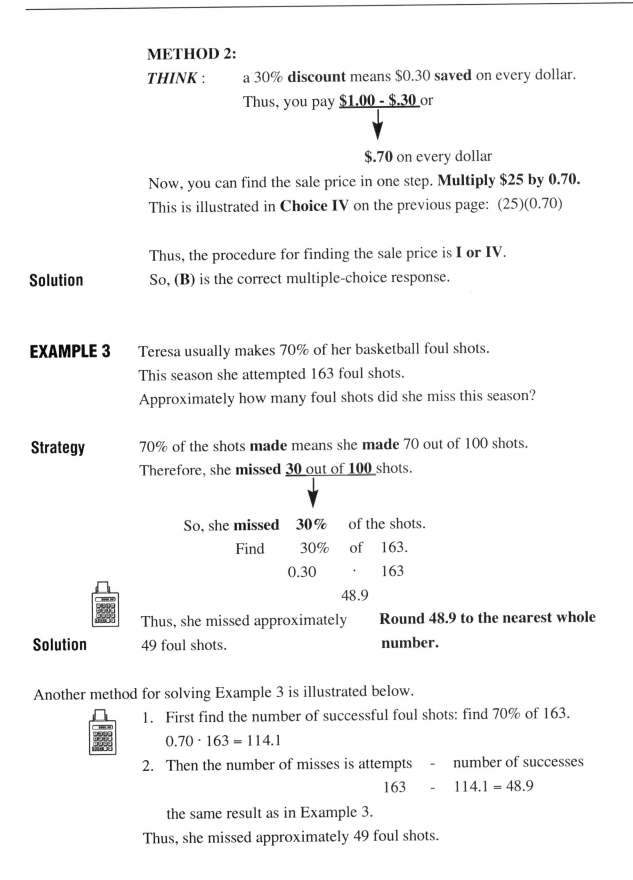

Thus, she missed approximately   **Round 48.9 to the nearest whole**

Solution   49 foul shots.   **number.**

Another method for solving Example 3 is illustrated below.

1. First find the number of successful foul shots: find 70% of 163.

0.70 · 163 = 114.1

2. Then the number of misses is attempts   -   number of successes

163   -   114.1 = 48.9

the same result as in Example 3.

Thus, she missed approximately 49 foul shots.

EXAMPLE 4 These price tags are for the same model stereo at two different stores. How much money is saved by buying at the lower price?

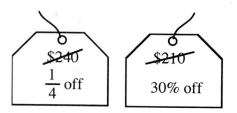

Strategy **Step 1** Find each discount.

Find $\frac{1}{4}$ of $240.   Find 30% of $210.

$240 ÷ 4 = $60   0.30 · $210 = $63

Step 2 Find the sale price of each stereo.

$240	$210
- 60	- 63
$180	$147

Step 3 Find the amount saved by buying the less expensive stereo.

$180   **more expensive**

- 147   **less expensive**

$ 33

Solution Thus, $33 is saved by buying the less expensive stereo.

EXAMPLE 5 Which of the following is **NOT** a way to find 125% of a number?

(A)   Multiply the number by 1.25.

(B)   Divide the number by 4 and add the result to the number.

(C)   Divide the number by 4 and multiply the result by 5.

(D)   Multiply the number by 0.25 and multiply the result by 4.

Strategy (A) is one way to find 125% of a number. (**125% = 1.25**)

Now rewrite 125% other ways.

$125\% = 1.25$

$= 1\frac{25}{100}$ **Write the decimal as a fraction.**

$= 1\frac{1}{4}$ **Reduce $\frac{25}{100}$ to lowest terms.**

$= \frac{5}{4}$ $1\frac{1}{4} = \frac{4 \cdot 1 + 1}{4}$

(continued on next page)

So, to find 125% of a number multiply be 1.25 **OR** $\frac{5}{4}$.

Multiplying by $\frac{5}{4}$ can be done by

1. multiplying by 5 and then dividing by 4, or
2. dividing by 4 and then multiplying by 5.

Thus, (C) is a second way to find 125% of a number.

This leaves one of the two remaining choices to **NOT** be a way.

Let's look at (B).

Think of **125%** as **100% + 25%**.

To find **125%** of a number,

find **100% of the number**   +   **25% of the number.**

number	added to	25% of the number
number	added to	$\frac{25}{100}$ of the number
number	added to	$\frac{1}{4}$ of the number
number	added to	number divided by 4

So, (B) is a third way to find 125% of a number.

Therefore, (A), (B), and (C) are all ways to find 125% of a number.

Solution   This leaves (D) as **NOT** a way to find 125% of a number.

Notice that the example above suggests several ways to find a percent **(larger than 100%)** of a number. For example, to find 150% of a number:

(1)   Multiply the number by 1.50.

(2) $150\% = 1.50 = 1\frac{50}{100} = 1\frac{1}{2} = \frac{3}{2}$

Multiply the number by 3 and divide the result by 2.

Divide the number by 2 and multiply the result by 3.

(3) $150\% = 100\% + 50\%$

Add the number to 50% of the number.

SUMMARY

1. How do you find 30% of 350?

How do you write each of the following percents as a decimal?

2. 3%   3. 300%

4. Mona had 25% of the answers wrong on a math test.
   How do you find the percent of correct answers?

5. You can find 125% of 60 by multiplying 60 by what decimal?

6. You can find 125% of 60 by adding __ to ___.

7. Explain how to find 125% of 60 by first converting 125% to a fraction.

8. A camera that regularly sells for $80 is on sale at a discount of 20%.
   What are two different ways to find the sale price?

9. What are two different ways to solve the following problem?
   Find the total cost of a $45 video game including a 6% sales tax.

10. How do you find out which is the better buy?
    Discount of $\frac{1}{4}$ off a regular $40 price **OR** 30% discount on a regular price of $35

SAMPLE EWT QUESTIONS

1. Find the total cost of a $500 stereo including a 6% sales tax.
   A. $30   B. $470   C. $506   D. $530

2. Find the sale price of a $50 camera if there is a 20% discount.
   A. $49.00   B. $40   C. $10   D. $1.00

3. Find the total cost of a $55 catchers mitt if there is an 8% sales tax.
   A. $4.40   B. $59.04   C. $59.40   D. $99.00

4. Find the sale price of a $300 television discounted at 25%.
   A. $75   B. $225   C. $325   D. $375

5. Deshonne got 20% of 40 questions wrong on a test. How many of her answers were correct?

    A. 8   B. 20   C. 30   D. 32

6. Julio usually makes 60% of his basketball shots. This season he attempted 149 foul shots. Approximately how many would he have been expected to miss?

    A. 40   B. 60   C. 89   D. 140

7. The basketball team won 75% of the 20 games played this season.
Find the number lost if there were no ties.

    A. 5   B. 15   C. 16   D. 25

8. Pierre wants to order a T-Shirt with "Pierre" printed on it. The T-shirt costs $7.99. Then there is a charge of $0.59 for each letter printed on it. Find the total cost including a 6% sales tax. (Round the final answer up to the nearest cent.)

    A. $3.76   B. $11.53   C. $9.10   D. $12.22

9. There are 40 questions on a test. What is the least number of correct answers needed to get a score of 70% on that test?

    A. 37   B. 33   C. 28   D. 12

10. A jacket was on sale at 35% off its price at Seaview Mall. The same type of jacket was 25% off its price at Paramus Mall. Tanya decided to buy the jacket at Seaview Mall. By buying there, would she have saved more than if she had purchased it at Paramus Mall?
    A. Yes, because the jacket costs 35% less at Seaview Mall.
    B. Yes, because a 35% savings is greater than a 25% savings.
    C. No, because the jacket was less expensive at Paramus Mall.
    D. Not necessarily, because the prices of the jackets may not have been the same at the two malls.

11. The eighth graders in one school collected toys for needy children. This year 80 students gave toys. This figure is 120% of what it was last year. This means that
    A. 20 more students gave toys this year than last year.
    B. the number of students giving toys decreased from last year to this year.
    C. 96 students gave toys last year.
    D. the number of students giving toys increased from last year to this year.

12. Super Games is selling a particular video game at $\frac{1}{5}$ off its regular price of $49. The same type of game is selling for 28% off its regular price of $54 at Video Outlet. At which of these stores is the video game less expensive, and by how much has it been reduced?

A. Video Outlet by $5.00

B. Video Outlet by $15.12

C. Super Games by $0.32

D. Super Games by $9.80

13. These price tags are from two stores for the same model television. What is the lower reduced price for this model television?

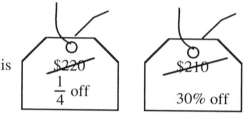

A. $63   B. $140

C. $147   D. $165

14. A Federal study found that in the Pine Barrens of New Jersey, 95% of the 800 streams and 60% of the 675 lakes tested in the study were acidic enough to cause damage to some aquatic life. How many of the lakes in the study were acidic enough to cause some damage to some aquatic life?

15. If you left a tip of 15% of the total of the bill including a 6% sales tax, what should the tip be, rounded to the nearest cent?

Tony's Deli
1 hamburger $4.50
1 grilled cheese $2.25
1 soda $0.85
1 milk $0.90
Tax   _____
Total   _____

16. Which of the following is **NOT** a way to find 140% of a number?

A. Multiply the number by 5 and then divide the result by 7.

B. Multiply the number by 0.40. Then add the result to the number.

C. Multiply the number by 7 and then divide the result by 5.

D. Multiply the number by 1.40.

17. Which of the following is a way to find 150% of 20?

I $0.15 \cdot 20$

II $20 + \frac{1}{2}$ of 20

III Multiply 20 by 3 and then divide the result by 2.

IV $1.50 \cdot 20$

A. II only
B. II or IV only
C. I or IV only
D. II, III, or IV only

18. A bicycle costs $85. Which of these processes could you use to find the total cost including a 7% sales tax?

I Multiply 85 by 0.07 and add the result to 85.
II Multiply 85 by 1.07.
III Multiply 85 by 0.93.
IV Multiply 85 by 0.07 and subtract the result from 85.

A. I only
B. II only
C. III or IV only
D. I or II only

19. If you found this same brand at **BETTER BUYS** for $79.90, which process below would you use to find the price that Don's Discount Store would charge you for the tape player?

DON'S DISCOUNT STORE

Buy Our Deluxe Tape Player for Only $89.90

If you can find this cheaper at any other store, we'll sell you a tape player for 10% less than our competitor's price for it.

I Multiply $79.90 by 0.1 and subtract the result from $79.90.
II Multiply $89.90 by 0.1 and subtract the result from $79.90.
III Multiply $89.90 by 0.9.
IV Multiply $79.90 by 0.9.

A. I only
B. II only
C. II or III only
D. I or IV only

OPEN-ENDED QUESTION

20.   A store manager instructed a clerk to advertise a $100 jacket at 10% discount. The following week the clerk was told to advertise the reduced jacket at a new 10% discount off its already reduced price. The clerk thought to himself that this was really the same as a total discount of 20% off the original price. Was the clerk right? Defend your conclusion with an actual numerical illustration.

REVIEW

1.   A six-pack of soda costs $2.70. Find the cost of one can.
   A. $0.40   B. $0.45   C. $2.76   D. $16.20

2.   Mark's scores on four tests are three 92's and one 88. Find his mean score.
   A. 88   B. 90   C. 91   D. 92

3.   Bill buys 5 pens at $0.30 each. Find the cost of the 5 pens including a 6% sales tax.
   A. $1.41   B. $1.50   C. $1.59   D. $15.90

4.   Masud packs 6 cassette tapes in a box. Since he began, he has packed a total of 95 tapes. Which box is now being packed?

   A. 5th   B. 15th   C. 16th   D. 17th

5.   Which of the following is a way to find $\frac{2}{3}$ of a number?
   A. Multiply the number by 2 and divide the result by 3.
   B. Multiply the number by 3 and divide the result by 2.
   C. Multiply the number by $\frac{3}{2}$.
   D. Divide the number by 2 and then divide the result by 3.

6.   Don ran 28 times around a quarter-mile track.
   How many miles did he run?

LESSON 5   NUMERICAL OPERATIONS
Number Properties

Some questions on the EWT require you to recognize whether a number is odd, even, prime, or factorable.

The numbers 0, 2, 4, 6, 8, 10, 12, etc. are **even** numbers.
Even numbers are divisible exactly by 2.

The numbers 1, 3, 5, 7, 9, 11, etc. are **odd** numbers.
Odd numbers are **not** divisible exactly by 2.

The product of $8 \cdot 4$ is 32.   8 and 4 are **factors** of 32.
Factors are numbers that are multiplied.

7 is a **prime** number.
The only whole numbers whose multiplication is 7 are **7** and **1**.
The only factors of 7 are 7 and 1.
A **prime** number is a whole number greater than 1 whose only factors are itself and 1.

EXAMPLE 1   What number has all the following characteristics?
- It is a prime number.
- It is greater than 20
- It is less than 30
- It does not have a 3 in its units (ones) place.

Strategy   First, list the whole numbers between 20 and 30:
   21, 22, 23, 24, 25, 26, 27,28, 29.
   Which of these are prime?
   23 and 29 have no factors other than 1.
   But 23 has a 3 in the units place.

Solution   This leaves 29 as the solution.

Numbers can be compared using **inequality** symbols.

For example, you know that 5 **is less than** 9.

$$\downarrow$$

$$5 < 9 \quad (< \text{ means "is less than"})$$

Similarly,   8 **is greater than** 3.

$$\downarrow$$

$$8 > 3 \quad (> \text{ means "is greater than"})$$

Think of a whole number between 5 and 8.

Let **x** represent this number.

"The whole number **x** is between 5 and 8" can be written as

$$5 < x < 8. \quad (5 \text{ is less than x, and x is less than 8})$$

$$\downarrow$$

The value of x could be **6**: $5 < 6 < 8$

The value of x could be **7**: $5 < 7 < 8$

EXAMPLE 2   Find x if x is prime and $4 < x < 9$.

Strategy   Since x is prime, x must represent a whole number.

THINK: What whole numbers are between 4 and 9?

       5, 6, 7, and 8 are between 4 and 9.

Which of these are prime?

5 and 7 are prime.   **5 has no factors other than 1 and 5.**

                                7 has no factors other than 1 and 7.

So there are two values of x that are each prime and between 4 and 9.

Solution   Thus, x = 5 or x = 7.

In an expression like 4^3, the **3** is called an **exponent**.

$$4^3 \text{ means } 4 \cdot 4 \cdot 4 \quad \textbf{(4 is used as a factor three times.)}$$

$$= 4 \cdot 16$$

$$= 64$$

$$4^3 \text{ is } \textbf{NOT } 12.$$

Similarly, $6^2 = 6 \cdot 6 = 36$.

An expression like 6^2 is read as "6 **squared**."

EXAMPLE 3   Which of the following numbers is **NOT** equal to the others?

A. $7 \cdot 3 - 5$ B. $9 \div \dfrac{1}{2}$

C. 2^4 D. $15 < x < 18$ and x is even

Strategy   Find the value of each.

A. $7 \cdot 3 - 5$ B. $9 \div \dfrac{1}{2}$

     21 - 5   **Multiply first.** $9 \cdot \dfrac{2}{1} = \dfrac{9}{1} \cdot \dfrac{2}{1}$

       16   **Then subtract.**   **18**

C. $2^4 = 2 \cdot 2 \cdot 2 \cdot 2$ D. x is even tells you x

     $= 4 \cdot 4$ is a whole number.

     $= $ **16**   16 and 17 are whole numbers

                                      between 15 and 18.

                                      But, **16** is the only even one.

Solution   Thus, the numbers are all 16 except for 18, choice **B**.

In arithmetic, addition can be **undone** by subtraction.

     For example, $2 + \mathbf{5} = 7$. $7 - \mathbf{5} = 2$

Adding 5 to 2 can be **undone** by subtracting 5 from 7.

Likewise, multiplication can be **undone** by division.

You have seen that an expression like 6^2 is interpreted as the **square of** 6.

     $6^2 = 6 \cdot 6 = 36$.

To **undo** squaring 6, find the **square root** of 36. (The symbol for **square root** is $\sqrt{}$.)

That is, you find a positive number which multiplied by itself is 36.

$$\sqrt{36} = 6,$$

since 6 is the positive number which multiplied by itself is 36.

Other examples of square roots are: $\sqrt{49} = 7$, since $7^2 = 7 \cdot 7 = 49$,

$\sqrt{64} = 8$, since $8^2 = 8 \cdot 8 = 64$.

EXAMPLE 4   Simplify $\sqrt{81}$

Solution $\sqrt{81} = 9$, since $9^2 = 81$

If there is no **exact** square root, then use a calculator as shown below.

$a = \sqrt{65}$

$a = 8.0622577$ **Enter 65. Press the $\sqrt{}$ key.**

EXAMPLE 5   Chang got an answer of about 4.90 when he entered 24 on his calculator and pressed the $\sqrt{}$ key. As usual, he stopped to think whether the calculator answer was reasonable.

Which of the following is the most likely explanation for him to believe that his calculator answer is or is not reasonable?

A.   It is not reasonable, because the answer should be a whole number.

B.   It is reasonable, because 4 squared is 16 while 5 squared is 25.

C.   It is not reasonable, because the answer should be only slightly more than 4.

D.   It is reasonable, because 4 and 24 are both even numbers.

Strategy   Estimate $\sqrt{24}$. Find positive numbers whose squares are close to 24.

$$3^2 = 9, \qquad 4^2 = 16, \qquad 5^2 = 25$$

24 is **between 16** and **25**.

So, $\sqrt{24}$ must be between **4** and **5**. This suggests (B) is the solution.

Checking the other answers:

A. is not possible since there is no whole number between 4 and 5.

C. is not possible since a number slightly more than 4 when squared is close to 16, **not** 24.

D. is irrelevant. For example, 6.23 is certainly not the square root of 24 even though **6** and **24** are both even numbers

Solution   Therefore, B. is the solution.

EXAMPLE 6 Which of these is the closest approximation to $\sqrt{3000}$?

A. 50   B. 60   C. 54.1   D. 54.7

Strategy You could square each multiple-choice answer to see which result is closest to 3000.

It is faster to use a calculator to find $\sqrt{3000}$.

Then determine which multiple-choice answer is closest to $\sqrt{3000}$.

Enter 3000. Press the $\sqrt{}$ key: Read 54.772256.

Solution The closest multiple-choice answer is **D**, 54.7.

When working with a calculator you have to be careful to press the corrrect key. Suppose, for example, you hit the multiplication key instead of the division key on a calculator. What should you do with the answer to undo the error?

Let's first try an easy illustration of the idea.

Suppose you want to divide 15 by 3. You should get **5** as an answer. Instead you make the mistake of **multiplying** 15 by 3.

You get $15 \cdot 3 = 45$.

You try to **undo** this by dividing 45 by 3. You get $45 \div 3 = 15$. This is **NOT** 5.

You must now divide 15 by 3 as you were asked to do in the beginning!

$15 \div 3 = \mathbf{5}$.

So, if you mistakenly **multiply** a number times 3 instead of dividing, you can get the right answer by **dividing** by 3 **twice!**

EXAMPLE 7 Kathy mistakenly multiplied by 15 instead of dividing by 15 while using her calculator. If the **in**correct answer displayed on the calculator is 90, what is the correct answer?

Strategy She first has to **UNDO** multiplication by 15. Multiplication is **UNDONE** by division.

So, first divide 90 by 15: $90 \div 15 = 6$.

But this is **NOT** the correct answer. 6 is the number she began with.

She was supposed to have **divided** 6 by 15.

$6 \div 15 = 0.4$.

Solution Therefore, the correct answer is 0.4.

SUMMARY

1. Give an example of a prime number. Why is it prime?

How do you read each of the following inequalities?

2. $7 > 3$ 3. $5 < 12$

4. For the expression 4^5, what number is the exponent?
   What does this exponent tell you to do?

5. How do you find x if x is odd and $7 < x < 12$?

6. How do you find $\sqrt{36}$ without using a calculator?

7. How do you find what two whole numbers $\sqrt{37}$ must be between?

8. How can you determine whether $\sqrt{5000}$ is closer to 80.5 or 70.7?

9. Suppose you mistakenly add 35 to a number instead of subtracting 35 from the number. If your result was 75, how could you find the correct answer?

SAMPLE EWT QUESTIONS

1. What number has all the following characteristics?
   - It is greater than 35
   - It is prime
   - It is less than 42
   - The units digit is less than 6.

2. What value of x makes $x < 8$ true?

   I $3\frac{1}{2}$ II 8   III 10   IV 7

   A. I only   B. I and IV only

   C. I, II , and IV only   D. IV only

3. What value of x makes $14 < x < 19$ true if x is odd but not prime?

   A. 18   B. 17   C. 16   D. 15

4. Simplify $\sqrt{16}$.

   A. 256   B. 32   C. 8   D. 4

-46-

5   Which of the numbers below is not equal to the other three?

A. $3 \cdot 2 + 1$ B. $\sqrt{36}$ C. $2^3 - 1$ D $2 \cdot 3\frac{1}{2}$

6.   Which of the numbers below is not equal to the other three?

A. $2.1 \cdot 10^2$ B. 210% C. $\frac{21}{10}$ D. $\sqrt{4.41}$

7.   Which of these choices could you write in the blank to make a true statement?

$$\sqrt{\frac{324}{729}} \underline{\hspace{1cm}} \frac{1}{3} \text{ of } 2$$

A. $<$ B. $>$ C. $=$ D. cannot be determined

(**HINT:** Use a calculator to evaluate $\sqrt{\frac{324}{729}}$:

Enter 324   enter $\div$ enter 729   enter $=$ enter $\sqrt{}$)

8.   Which of the numbers below is not equal to the other three?

A. $\frac{329.4}{658.8}$ B. $\sqrt{\frac{1107}{4428}}$ C. $\frac{2}{16}$ D. $\frac{2}{3} - \frac{1}{6}$

9.   Juan got an answer of 6.0827625 when he used his calculator to find $\sqrt{37}$.
He decided to check the reasonableness of his answer. Which of the following
is the most likely explanation for him to believe that his calculator answer is or is not
reasonable?
A. It is not reasonable, because the answer should only be a little less than 7.
B. It is reasonable, because 6 squared is 36 and 7 squared is 49.
C. It is not reasonable, because the answer should be a whole number.
D. It is reasonable, because 6 is an even number.

10.   You can estimate $\sqrt{85}$ as being between which two numbers below?
A. 7 and 8   B. 8 and 9   C. 9 and 10   D. 10 and 11

11.   Which of these is the closest approximation to $\sqrt{4300}$?

A. 55.6   B. 60.6   C. 65.6   D. 70.6

12.   Joan mistakenly divided by 18 instead of multiplying by 18 when using her calculator.
If the incorrect answer displayed on the calculator is 3, what is the correct answer?

A. 972   B. 54   C. 15   D. 6

13. Rudy was supposed to subtract 119 from a number. By mistake, he added 119 and got 247. What is the correct answer?

    A. 9   B. 19   C. 128   D. 366

14. Which of the following is not equal to the other three?

    A. $\frac{1}{5}$ of 50   B. $5 \cdot \sqrt{4}$ C. $2 \div \frac{1}{5}$ D. 30% of 20

15. What prime number is between 11 and 17?

16. What value of x makes $12 < x < 17$ if x is odd and its units digit is not 5?

17. The numbers 7 and 8 are **consecutive**. Two whole numbers are consecutive if they differ by 1. $\sqrt{65}$ is between what two consecutive numbers?

18. Simplify $(\frac{3}{4})^2$.

19. Jaime was supposed to find the square root of a number. By mistake she pressed the x^2 key, which **squared** the number. The calculator answer was therefore 331776. What should the correct answer be?

OPEN-ENDED QUESTION

20. Simplify each of the following: $(\sqrt{49})^2$ $(\sqrt{64})^2$ $(\sqrt{81})^2$.

Predict the value of $(\sqrt{345.6})^2$ without using a calculator. Explain why this works.

REVIEW

1. Use this advertisement to find the cost of a $6\frac{1}{2}$ minute call.

    A. $3.50

    B. $8.25

    C. $9.00

    D. $11.00

KEEP UP WITH SPORTS
Find out what happenend in your favorite sport yesterday. DIAL 1-900-999-1234. Your phone company will bill you $2.00 for the first minute and $1.50 for each additional minute and partial minute.

2.   Marla plans to purchase a sleeping bag advertised at $74.89. She uses her calculator to find the 7% sales tax. Her calculator displays 5.2423. Assuming that prices are rounded up to the nearest cent, find the total amount, including sales tax, she will be charged.
    A. $80.13   B. $80.14   C. $80.89   D. $80.90

3.   A basketball team won 75% of the 20 games played. How many games were lost?

    A. 15   B. 14   C. 6   D. 5

4.   Which of the following is **NOT** a way to find 150% of a number?

    A. Multiply the number by 1.50.
    B. Add half of the number to the number.
    C. Multiply the number by 3, then divide the result by 2.
    D. Divide the number by 3, then multiply the result by 2.

5.   Which of the following is the best buy for soda cans?
    A. 3 for $2.26   B. one dozen for $6.00
    C. 4 for $2.24   D. 6-pack for $3.32

6.   A radio costs $75. Which of these procedures could you use to find the total cost including a 6% sales tax?
              I   Multiply 75 by 0.06 and subtract the result from 75.
              II   Multiply 75 by 0.94.
              III   Multiply 75 by 1.06.
              IV   Multiply 75 by 0.06 and add the result to 75.
    A. II only   B. III only
    C. III or IV only   D. I only

7.   Video Shack is selling a video game at $\frac{1}{4}$ off its regular $48.00 price. At Bargain Videos, the same game is selling at 26% off its regular price of $52 At which store is that the game less expensive, and by how much has it been reduced at that store?

-49-

There are 68 girls and 59 boys in the eighth grade. Many of them are taking a foreign language.

Answer Questions 8–11 based on information in the table.

FOREIGN LANGUAGE ENROLLMENT		
Course	Girls	Boys
Spanish	35	25
French	21	19
German	12	15

8. How many more girls than boys are in Spanish classes?

9. The number of boys in Spanish is how much more than the number of girls in German?

10. Find the average of the number of boys in foreign-language courses.

11. How many eighth-grade girls are not taking any foreign language?

12. In our school, the girls soccer team won $\frac{4}{5}$ of the 15 games played this season. How many games were lost if there were no ties?

LESSON 6 NUMERICAL OPERATIONS
Fractions

The fraction $\frac{8}{4}$ has the same value as $8 \div 4 = 2$.

You can interpret $\frac{3}{4}$ as $3 \div 4$.

So, $\frac{3}{4} = 0.75$

$$\begin{array}{r} 0.750 \\ 4\overline{)3.000} \end{array}$$

Similarly, $\frac{5}{8} = 0.625$

$$\begin{array}{r} 0.625 \\ 8\overline{)5.000} \end{array}$$

Notice in the illustrations above, each decimal **ends** or **terminates**.

EXAMPLE 1   Write the fraction $\frac{5}{7}$ as a decimal. As you carry out the division, what pattern do you discover? (Carry out the division 18 places.)

Strategy   Divide 7 into 5.000000 000000 000000

$$\begin{array}{r} 0.714285\ 714285\ 714285 \\ 7\overline{)5.000000\ 000000\ 000000} \end{array}$$

The quotient (answer) **repeats** in blocks of 6 digits.
The block **714285** repeats forever.

Solution   The decimal $\frac{5}{7}$ is called a **repeating** decimal.

Every simple fraction can be written as either a **terminating** or a **repeating** decimal.
Every whole number is also a **terminating** or a **repeating** decimal.

EXAMPLE 2   Determine whether the decimal for each simple fraction is repeating or terminating:

(A) $\frac{1}{4}$

$$\begin{array}{r} 0.25 \\ 4\overline{)1.00} \end{array}$$

(B) $\frac{2}{3}$

$$\begin{array}{r} 0.666 \\ 3\overline{)2.000} \end{array}$$

Solution   0.25 is a **terminating** decimal.

0.666 is a **repeating** decimal.

You could have used a calculator to solve Example 2 of the previous page.

For example, to write $\frac{2}{3}$ as a decimal:

Enter 2   Enter ÷   Enter 3   Enter =   Read   0.6666667

Note, however, that entering 2 ÷ 3 produces the result 0.6666667.

The calculator **rounded** the last digit, since there was no room to display more digits on the screen.

In reality, the decimal does **repeat** .

The EWT will ask you to predict many kinds of **patterns**.

One kind of pattern involves **repeating** decimals. The next example asks you to use the pattern of a repeating decimal to predict which digit will be in an indicated decimal place.

EXAMPLE 3   What digit is in the seventieth decimal place when $\frac{5}{7}$ is written as a decimal?

Strategy   First write $\frac{5}{7}$ as a decimal as shown in Example 1 on the previous page.

$$\overline{7)5.000000\ 000000\ 000000} \ \ 0.\overline{714285\ 714285\ 714285}$$

The **block** of 6 symbols **714285** repeats.

How many **6's** are there in 70? Divide 70 by 6.

The block of symbols **714285** repeats 11 times with **4** symbols left over.

The **4th** symbol in the block 714285 is **2**.

$$\begin{array}{r} 11 \\ 6)\overline{70} \\ 6 \\ \hline 10 \\ 6 \\ \hline 4 \end{array}$$

Solution   Therefore, **2** is in the seventieth place.

EXAMPLE 4   Which of the fractions greater than 1, below, has all three of the following characteristics?
- It is less than 2.
- It represents a non-terminating (repeating) decimal.
- It has a 6 in the tenths place when written in decimal form.

A. $\frac{5}{3}$ B. $\frac{14}{12}$ C. $\frac{16}{6}$ D. $\frac{8}{5}$ (**solution on next page**)

Strategy

First use a calculator to write each fraction in decimal form.

$$\frac{5}{3} = 1.6666667$$

$$\frac{14}{12} = 1.1666667 \quad \textbf{(repeats after 1.1)}$$

$$\frac{16}{6} = 2.6666667$$

$$\frac{8}{5} = 1.6000000$$

Form a **TABLE** displaying the 4 improper **fractions** and the three **characteristics**.

	less than 2	repeating decimal	has a 6 in tenths place
$\frac{5}{3} = \textbf{1.6666667}$	**yes**	**yes**	**yes**
$\frac{14}{12} = 1.1666667$	yes	yes	no **(1 in tenths place)**
$\frac{16}{6} = 2.6666667$	no **(more than 2)**	yes	yes
$\frac{8}{5} = 1.6000000$	yes	no **(term. dec.)**	yes

Only the first row has a **yes** in all **three categories** or columns.

Solution

Therefore, choice A, $\frac{5}{3}$, is the solution.

Sometimes it is easier to **compare** two fractions by first rewriting them as decimals.

EXAMPLE 5

Which of these symbols would produce a true statement if written in the blank?

$$7\frac{3}{8} \underline{\quad\quad} 7\frac{3}{5}$$

A. <　　　　B. =　　　C. >　　　D. none of these

Strategy

Rewrite each fraction as a decimal.

$$\frac{3}{8} = 0.\textbf{3}750000 \qquad \frac{3}{5} = 0.\textbf{6}000000$$

Now　　7.**3**750000　　<　　7.**6**000000

Solution

So,　　　　$7\frac{3}{8} < 7\frac{3}{5}$, Choice A.

Sometimes it is helpful to compare two fractions by rewriting them so that they have the **same**, or a **common**, denominator.

Usually it is convenient to find the **Least Common Denominator (LCD)**.

To rewrite $\frac{5}{6}$ and $\frac{3}{4}$ with the same LCD:

1. Find the **smallest** number divisible by both 6 and 4. It is 12.
2. Rewrite each fraction with a denominator of 12.

$$\frac{5}{6} = \frac{5 \cdot 2}{6 \cdot 2} = \frac{10}{12}$$

Think: 6 · ? = 12?

Multiply numerator and denominator by 2.

$$\frac{3}{4} = \frac{3 \cdot 3}{4 \cdot 3} = \frac{9}{12}$$

Think: 4 · ? = 12?

Multiply numerator and denominator by 3.

Notice the following relationship for fractions on a number line.

$\frac{3}{4}$ is greater than $\frac{1}{2}$.

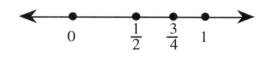

The **bigger** of two fractions between 0 and 1 is **closer to 1.**

The **smaller** of two fractions between 0 and 1 is **closer to 0.**

The next example uses the method of deciding which of two fractions is closer to 0 or 1 in order to determine which fraction is bigger.

EXAMPLE 6   Mr. Johnson asked students in his class to explain why $\frac{5}{6}$ is greater than $\frac{3}{4}$.

Which of these is the correct response to Mr. Johnson's request?

A. because, on a number line, $\frac{5}{6}$ is closer to 1 than $\frac{3}{4}$ is

B. because, on a number line, $\frac{5}{6}$ is closer to 0 than $\frac{3}{4}$ is

C. because 5 is greater than 3

D. because 6 is greater than 4

Strategy   Multiple Choices A and B compare the fractions with 0 and 1 on a number line. So you must first find which fraction is bigger.

Then you must see their relationship to 0 and 1 on a number line.

(continued on next page)

First rewrite $\frac{5}{6}$, $\frac{3}{4}$, and 1 all with the same denominator as shown on the previous page.

$$\frac{5}{6} = \frac{10}{12} \qquad \frac{3}{4} = \frac{9}{12} \qquad 1 = \frac{12}{12}$$

Now, since all three fractions have the same denominator, 12, you can use the **numerators** to write the fractions in order from smallest to largest.

You can see that $\frac{10}{12} > \frac{9}{12}$.

But the multiple choices refer to a number line!

Show the numbers on a number line. You can see that $\frac{10}{12}$ is closer to 1 than $\frac{9}{12}$.

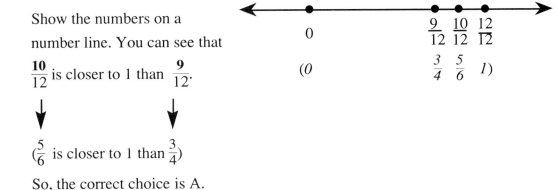

$(\frac{5}{6}$ is closer to 1 than $\frac{3}{4})$

Solution   So, the correct choice is A.

If two fractions have **unlike** denominators, such as $\frac{5}{6}$ and $\frac{3}{4}$ above, you **CANNOT** conclude that $\frac{5}{6}$ is larger than $\frac{3}{4}$ by saying that 5 is larger than 3.

Compare fractions only if their **denominators** are the same.

$\frac{5}{9} < \frac{7}{9}$ since the denominators are the same and 5 < 7.

$\frac{7}{10} > \frac{3}{10}$ since their denominators are the same and 7 > 3.

The next example asks you to insert two fractions between $\frac{1}{4}$ and $\frac{1}{2}$.

This would be easier if the original fractions had the same denominator.

For example, two fractions between $\frac{3}{7}$ and $\frac{6}{7}$ are $\frac{4}{7}$ and $\frac{5}{7}$.

THINK: $\frac{3}{7}, \frac{4}{7}, \frac{5}{7}, \frac{6}{7}$.

EXAMPLE 7   Insert two fractions between $\frac{1}{4}$ and $\frac{1}{2}$.

Strategy   First, rewrite so that the fractions have the same denominator.

1. Find the smallest number divisible by both 2 and 4. It is 4.
2. Rewrite each fraction with a denominator of 4.

$$\frac{1}{2} = \frac{1 \cdot 2}{2 \cdot 2} = \frac{2}{4}$$

$$\frac{1}{4}$$

You want two fractions between $\frac{1}{4}$ and $\frac{2}{4}$.

But, there is no whole number between **1** and **2**.

Rewrite each fraction.

Multiply numerator and denominator of each fraction by 2.

$$\frac{1 \cdot 2}{4 \cdot 2} = \frac{2}{8} \qquad\qquad \frac{2 \cdot 2}{4 \cdot 2} = \frac{4}{8}$$

You now want two fractions between $\frac{2}{8}$ and $\frac{4}{8}$.

But, there is only **one whole** number between **2** and **4**. You want **two** of them!

Try rewriting $\frac{2}{4}$ and $\frac{1}{4}$ by multiplying numerator and denominator of each by **3**.

$$\frac{1 \cdot 3}{4 \cdot 3} = \frac{3}{12} \qquad\qquad \frac{2 \cdot 3}{4 \cdot 3} = \frac{6}{12}$$

There are **two** whole numbers between **3** and **6**: **4** and **5**.

Two fractions between $\frac{3}{12}$ and $\frac{6}{12}$ are $\frac{4}{12}$ and $\frac{5}{12}$.

Solution   Two fractions between $\frac{1}{4}$ and $\frac{1}{2}$ are $\frac{4}{12}$ and $\frac{5}{12}$, or

$$\downarrow$$

$\frac{1}{3}$ and $\frac{5}{12}$.   **Reduce $\frac{4}{12}$ to $\frac{1}{3}$.**

When approximating sums of fractions, it may be easier to convert each fraction to a decimal and round the results than to rewrite each with the same LCD. This is illustrated in the next example.

EXAMPLE 8   Which of these whole numbers most closely approximates the sum of

$$4\frac{7}{9} + 5\frac{1}{6} + 7\frac{4}{5}?$$

A. 16   B. 17   C. 18   D. 19

Strategy   First rewrite each as a decimal using a calculator.

Then round each to the nearest whole number.

$$\frac{7}{9} = 7 \div 9 = 0.7777778 \qquad \frac{1}{6} = 1 \div 6 = 0.1666667 \qquad \frac{4}{5} = 4 \div 5 = 0.8000000$$

$$4\frac{7}{9} = \boxed{4.7777778} \qquad 5\frac{1}{6} = \boxed{5.1666667} \qquad 7\frac{4}{5} = \boxed{7.8000000}$$

5 (rounded)   **5** (rounded)   **8** (rounded)

Thus, $4\frac{7}{9} + 5\frac{1}{6} + 7\frac{4}{5}$ is approximately **5 + 5 + 8**, or 18.

Solution   The correct answer choice is therefore **C**.

EXAMPLE 9   Tina purchased stock at \$$2\frac{3}{4}$ a share and sold it at \$$4\frac{3}{8}$ a share.
What was her profit on each share of that stock?

Strategy   The profit is the **difference** between what she paid and what she sold it for.
Subtract the two numbers: $4\frac{3}{8} - 2\frac{3}{4}$.

First find the LCD for the two fractions.

1. Find the smallest number divisible by both 4 and 8. It is 8.
2. Rewrite each number with a denominator of 8.

$$4\frac{3}{8} = \quad 4\frac{3}{8} \quad = \quad 4\frac{3}{8} \quad = \quad 3 + 1 + \frac{3}{8} \quad = \quad 3 + \frac{8}{8} + \frac{3}{8} \quad = \quad 3\frac{11}{8}$$

$$-2\frac{3}{4} = \quad -2\frac{3 \cdot 2}{4 \cdot 2} \quad = \quad -2\frac{6}{8} \quad = \quad -2\frac{6}{8} \quad = \quad -2\frac{6}{8} \quad = \quad -2\frac{6}{8}$$

$$1\frac{5}{8}$$

Solution   Thus, the profit is \$$1\frac{5}{8}$.

SUMMARY

1. What is a repeating decimal? Give an example.

2. What is a terminating decimal? Give an example.

3. How do you write the fraction $\frac{2}{7}$ as a decimal? Does it repeat or terminate?

4. How do you find what digit is in the fortieth decimal place of 0.45632 45632 45632?

5. How do you find out which of the two fractions $\frac{4}{7}$ and $\frac{3}{5}$ is the larger?

6. Two fractions are between 0 and 1. Which one is closer to 0? Which one is closer to 1?

7. How do you insert two fractions between $\frac{1}{5}$ and $\frac{1}{3}$?

8. How can you approximate the sum $3\frac{5}{7} + 4\frac{2}{11} + 8\frac{5}{9}$?

SAMPLE EWT QUESTIONS

1. Which of the following is a repeating decimal?

    A. $\frac{4}{5}$ B. $\frac{8}{9}$ C. $\frac{1}{8}$ D. $\frac{3}{4}$

2. Which of the following is a repeating decimal?

    A. $\frac{7}{8}$ B. $\frac{4}{5}$ C. $\frac{2}{3}$ D. $\frac{1}{4}$

3. What digit is in the thirtieth decimal place when $\frac{3}{7}$ is written as a decimal?

    A. 1   B. 5   C. 7   D. 8

4. What digit is in the twenty-fifth decimal place when $\frac{2}{11}$ is written as a decimal?

    A. 1   B. 2   C. 8   D. 9

5. Which of the fractions below has all three of the following characteristics?
    *   It is less than 1.
    *   It has a 5 in the tenths place when written in decimal form.
    *   It represents a repeating decimal.

    A. $\frac{9}{5}$ B. $\frac{5}{4}$ C. $\frac{8}{12}$ D. $\frac{4}{7}$

6. Which of the fractions below has all three of the following characteristics?

- It is greater than 1.
- It represents a terminating decimal.
- It has a 5 in the hundredths place.

    A. $\frac{3}{7}$ B. $\frac{5}{9}$ C. $\frac{11}{8}$ D. $\frac{9}{4}$

7. Which of these symbols would produce a true statement if written in the blank?

$$6\frac{5}{8} \underline{\quad} 6\frac{5}{9}$$

    A. <   B. =   C. >   D. none of these

8. Which of these symbols would produce a true statement if written in the blank?

$$8\frac{4}{9} \underline{\quad} \frac{3}{11}$$

    A. <   B. =   C. >   D. none of these

9. Which of the reasons below explains why $\frac{2}{3}$ is less than $\frac{5}{6}$?

    A. 2 is less than 5.   B. 3 is less than 6.

    C. $\frac{2}{3}$ is closer to 1 than $\frac{5}{6}$.   D. $\frac{2}{3}$ is closer to 0 than $\frac{5}{6}$.

10. Which of these whole numbers most closely approximates $6\frac{5}{6} + 8\frac{1}{3} + 9\frac{5}{7}$?

    A. 26   B. 25   C. 24   D. 23

11. Which of these whole numbers most closely approximates $4\frac{8}{9} + 7\frac{5}{8} + 6\frac{3}{4}$?

    A. 17   B. 18   C. 19   D. 20

12. Insert two fractions between $\frac{1}{3}$ and $\frac{5}{6}$.   13. Insert two fractions between $\frac{2}{3}$ and $\frac{1}{2}$.

14. Add: $2\frac{4}{5} + 3\frac{1}{2}$.   15. Subtract: $4\frac{1}{4} - 2\frac{1}{2}$.

16. The republics of the former Soviet Union produce about $\frac{1}{3}$ of the world's crude oil. The Middle East countries produce about $\frac{1}{2}$ of the world's crude oil. Find the combined oil production of these two regions.

OPEN-ENDED QUESTIONS

17. Explain how the number line can be used to justify which of the numbers $\frac{5}{8}$ and $\frac{3}{4}$ is the larger.

18. Example 8 showed how to round the fractions for estimating the sum by changing them to decimal form. There is another way to estimate the sum of several fractions.

    Consider $4\frac{7}{9}$. To round $4\frac{7}{9}$ to the nearest whole number, you must determine whether $\frac{7}{9}$ is less than, greater than, or equal to 0.5. But, $0.5 = \frac{1}{2}$.

    You can do this by determining whether 7 is more than, less than, or equal to half of 9. Now use this idea to explain how to estimate $3\frac{5}{7} + 6\frac{2}{11} + 5\frac{10}{13}$ without changing the fractions to decimal form.

REVIEW

1. A farmer owned $38\frac{1}{2}$ acres of farmland. He decided to give each of his three children an equal share when he retired. Which expression below can be used to determine the number of acres of land that he gave to each of his three children when he retired?

   A. $3\frac{1}{2} \cdot 3$ B. $38\frac{1}{2} \cdot \frac{1}{3}$ C. $38\frac{1}{2} - \frac{1}{3}$ D. none

2. Which of the following is the closest approximation to $\sqrt{3000}$?
   A. 15.00   B. 54.0   C. 54.8   D. 60.1

3. Which of the numbers below is not equal to the other three?
   A. 125%   B. $\sqrt{\frac{25}{16}}$ C. $1.25 \cdot 10^2$ D. $5 \div 4$

4. A team won 30% of the 20 games played. There were no ties. How many games did the team lose?

LESSON 7   PRE-ALGEBRA
Variables and Evaluation

A mathematical pattern frequently suggests a new concept.

What is the pattern below?

$$6 \cdot 2 + 7$$
$$6 \cdot 3 + 7$$
$$6 \cdot 4 + 7$$
$$6 \cdot 5 + 7$$

In each of the above expressions, the number multiplied by 6 changes or **VARIES**.

A letter like **n**, can be used to represent the **number** that changes or **VARIES**.

For example, 6 times a **number** plus 3 becomes

$$6 \cdot \mathbf{n} \quad + \quad 3, \text{ or} \qquad \text{(When multiplying by a variable, the}$$
$$6\mathbf{n} + 3 \qquad\qquad\qquad \text{raised dot can be dropped.)}$$

The **n** is called a **variable.**

A **variable** is a letter that can be replaced by a number.

The value of **6n + 3** depends upon the number that is substituted for the **variable n.**
This is illustrated in Example 1 below.

EXAMPLE 1   Evaluate 6n + 3 for n = 7.

Strategy   To "**evaluate** 6n + 3 for n = 7" means to replace n by 7 and then
compute the result.

$$6n + 3$$
$$6 \cdot \ n + 3 \qquad\qquad \textbf{6n means 6 times n or 6} \cdot \textbf{n.}$$

$$6 \cdot 7 + 3 \qquad\qquad \textbf{Replace n by 7. (Or substitute 7 for n.)}$$
$$42 \ + 3 \qquad\qquad \textbf{Use Order of Operations. Multiply first.}$$

Solution   45   **Then add.**

The next example provides a data table.

You are given values of x and y.

You will be asked to find the relationship between x and y.

EXAMPLE 2   What group of numbers correctly completes this table?

x	4(3 + x)
1	16
2	
6	
9	

Strategy   You are asked to **evaluate** 4(3 + x) for each given value of **x**: **2**, **6**, and **9**.

Replace **x** by **2**.

$4(3 + \mathbf{x})$

$\downarrow$

$4(3 + \mathbf{2})$

$4 \cdot 5$

Replace **x** by **6**.

$4(3 + \mathbf{x})$

$\downarrow$

$4(3 + \mathbf{6})$

$4 \cdot 9$

Replace **x** by **9**.

$4(3 + \mathbf{x})$

$\downarrow$

$4(3 + \mathbf{9})$

$4 \cdot 12$

Solution   20   36   48

EXAMPLE 3   Which of these equations is satisfied by the numbers in this table?

x	0	2	4	8
y	4	8	12	20

A. y = x + 4   B. y = 4 - x

C. y = 2x - 4   D. y = 2x + 4

Strategy   You are given 4 choices. In this case, try evaluation of each until you find one that works for all x and y values in the table

First check y = x + 4.

Does **y** = **4** when **x** = **0**?

Replace **x** by **0**, **y** by 4.

y = **x** + 4

4 = **0** + 4

4 = **4**   **YES**

Does **y** = **8** when **x** = **2**?

Replace **x** by **2**, **y** by **8**.

y = **x** + 4

8 = **2** + 4

8 = 6 **NO**

When **x** = 2, **y** = **8**.

x	0	**2**	4	8
y	4	**8**	12	20

Now check y = 4 - x.

It checks for **x** = **0** and **y** = **4**. (Check on your own.)

Does **y** = **8** when **x** = **2**?

Replace **x** by **2**, **y** by **8**.

y = **4** - **x**

8 = 4 - **2**

8 = 2   **NO**

When **x** = 0, **y** = **4**.

x	**0**	2	4	8
y	**4**	8	12	20

When **x** = 2, **y** = **8**.

x	0	**2**	4	8
y	4	**8**	12	20

(continued on next page)

Next you should check y = 2x - 4.

That also does **NOT** check for all values of x and y.

Finally, check **y = 2x + 4.**

You will find that only this equation checks for all

values of x and y.

We show the work only for

x = 4 and **y = 12**

Replace **x** by **4**, **y** by **12.**

When **x = 4, y = 12** .

x	0	2	**4**	8
y	4	8	**12**	20

$y = 2x + 4$

$12 = 2 \cdot 4 + 4$

$12 = 8 + 4$

$12 = 12$ **YES**

Check the other values of x and y on your own.

Solution   Thus, the answer is choice **D**, y = 2x + 4.

Evaluations sometimes involve exponents. Recall that 6^2 means $6 \cdot 6$.

So, n^2 means $n \cdot n$.

EXAMPLE 4   What value of n completes this table?

n	$n^2 + 5$
1	6
2	9
3	14
8	

Strategy   You are asked to **evaluate** $n^2 + 5$ for **b = 8.**

Replace **n** by **8.**

$n^2 + 5$

$8^2 + 5$

$8 \cdot 8 + 5$

$64 + 5$ **Multiply first. Then add.**

69

Solution   Thus, 69 is the value needed to complete the table.

SUMMARY

1. How do you evaluate 5x + 4 for x = 6?
2. How do you simplify $5^2 + 4$?
3. How do you evaluate 5(7 - x) for x = 2?
4. For x = 5, y = ?
5. How do you determine if the equation y = 3x + 2 is satisfied by the numbers of this table?

x	1	4	5	6	12
y	5	14	17	20	38

SAMPLE EWT QUESTIONS

Evaluate each for the given value of the variable.

1. 7n + 3 for n = 2
   A. 12   B. 17
   C. 27   D. 42

2. 5x - 2 for x = 4
   A. 7   B. 11
   C. 18   D. 22

3. 6 + 3k for k = 5
   A. 90   B. 48
   C. 21   D. 14

4. $x^2 + 7$ for x = 3
   A. 13   B. 16
   C. 42   D. 63

5. $18 - a^2$ for a = 4
   A. 2   B. 10
   C. 26   D. 34

6. $x^3 + 4$ for x = 2
   A. 10   B. 12
   C. 22   D. 24

What group of numbers correctly completes each table?

7.

x	5(2 + x)
1	15
3	
4	
9	

A. 30, 40, 90
B. 18, 22, 54
C. 25, 30, 16
D. 25, 30, 55

8.

x	2(x - 5)
7	4
8	
9	
10	

A. 6, 8, 10
B. 11, 13, 15
C. 5, 6, 7
D. 21, 23, 25

9.

x	$x^2 + 5$
1	6
2	
6	
9	

A. 20, 180, 405
B. 9, 17, 23
C. 9, 41, 86
D. 9, 60, 90

10. Which of these equations is satisfied by the numbers in this table?

x	0	2	4	6
y	6	10	14	18

A. $y = x + 6$ B. $y = 2x - 6$

C. $y = 6 - x$ D. $y = 2x + 6$

11. Which of these equations is satisfied by the numbers in this table?

x	0	3	4	7
y	5	14	17	26

A. $y = x + 5$ B. $y = 5 + 3x$

C. $y = 3x - 5$ D. $y = 4x + 2$

Evaluate each of the following for the given value of the variable.

12. $4 + 7m$ for $m = 3$ 13. $2(x + 5)$ for $x = 8$ 14. $7 + x^2$ for $x = 3$

What numbers correctly complete each table?

15.

x	5(3 + x)
1	20
2	
3	
6	

16.

x	3(5x - 1)
1	12
2	
6	
9	

17.

x	$x^2 - 2$
3	7
5	
7	
9	

Evaluate each of the following for the given value of the variable.

18. $35x + 119$ for $x = 39$

19. $243.5x - 123.775$ for $x = 0.92$

OPEN-ENDED QUESTION

20. Write an equation that relates x and y in this table.

x	2	3	4	5
y	5	7	9	11

HINT: y = some number times x + another number.

REVIEW

1. The weights of 4 bags of potato chips are given below. Which bag weighs the most?

   A. $\frac{3}{4}$ oz   B. $\frac{5}{8}$ oz   C. $\frac{1}{2}$ oz   D. $\frac{9}{16}$ oz

2. What digit is in the 29th decimal place when $\frac{6}{7}$ is written as a decimal?

   A. 1   B. 2   C. 3   D. 4

3. Which of the fractions below has all three of the following characteristics?

   • It is less than $\frac{1}{2}$

   • It represents a terminating decimal.

   • It has a 5 in the thousandths place when written as a decimal.

   A. $\frac{3}{8}$ B. $\frac{5}{4}$ C. $\frac{6}{11}$ D. $\frac{7}{8}$

4. Which of these symbols would produce a true statement if written in the blank?

   $$9\frac{5}{7} \underline{\quad} 9\frac{4}{5}$$

   A. <   B. >   C. =   D. none of these

5. Which of these whole numbers most closely approximates $5\frac{5}{6} + 4\frac{3}{8} + 7\frac{8}{9}$?

   A. 16   B. 17   C. 18   D. 19

6. Which of the numbers below is **NOT** equal to the other 3?

   A. 120%   B. $1.2 \cdot 10^2$ C. $\frac{6}{5}$ D. $\sqrt{1.44}$

7. Insert two fractions between $\frac{3}{4}$ and $\frac{1}{2}$.

8. Wanda purchased stock at $3\frac{3}{4}$ a share and sold it at $5\frac{1}{2}$ a share. What was her profit on 2 shares of that stock?

9. Find the sale price of a $40 camera if there is a 30% discount.

10. Tom ran exactly 24 times around a quarter-mile track. How many miles did he run?

11. Find the average of the following bowling scores: 250, 175, 210, 300, and 175.

LESSON 8   PRE-ALGEBRA
Number Lines, Adding Signed Numbers

Some questions on the EWT refer to number lines.

The number line below shows the following:

zero: the number corresponding to the point called the **origin,**

negative numbers to the left of zero,

positive numbers to the right of zero.

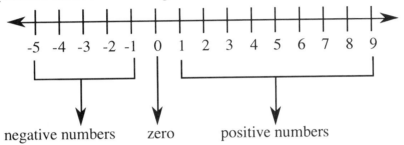

Point R has **coordinate** 2.

The **coordinate** of Q is -3.5.

The **coordinate** of P is -5.

Inequalities can be used to describe the relationship between two integers.

On the number line above, 2 < 6.   On the number line, 8 > 3.

Notice that 2 is to the **left** of 6.   Notice that 8 is to the **right** of 3.

On a number line: Numbers to the **left** of a number are **less** than that number.

Numbers to the **right** of a number are **greater** than that number.

EXAMPLE 1   Insert the appropriate inequality symbol to make each statement true.

-4 ? 3   -5 ? -1   3 ? -5

Strategy

-4 < 3   -5 < -1   3 > -5

-4 is to the **left** of 3   -5 is to the **left** of -1   3 is to the **right** of -5

-67-

You can insert the proper inequality between two integers without using a number line.
Think in terms of temperatures.

For example, -7 ? 4.

7° **below zero** is **colder** than 4° **above zero**.

7° **below zero** is a **lesser** temperature than 4° **above zero**.

Therefore, -7 < 4

As another example, consider -14 ? -13.

14° below zero is **colder** than 13° below zero.

14° below zero is a **lesser** temperature than 13° below zero.

Therefore, -14 < -13.

EXAMPLE 2   Insert the appropriate inequality symbol to make -2.482 __ -2.481 true.

Strategy   Think again in terms of temperatures.

2.48**2**° below 0   is **colder** than   2.48**1**° below 0.

Solution   Therefore, -2.482 < -2.481.

As another example, consider -18 ? -19

18° below zero is **warmer** than 19° below zero.

18° below zero is a **greater** temperature than 19° below zero.

Therefore, -18 > -19.

EXAMPLE 3   Insert the appropriate inequality symbol to make -3.56 __ -3.57 true.

Strategy   Think again in terms of temperatures.

3.56° below 0 is **warmer** than 3.57° below 0.

Solution   Therefore, -3.56 > -3.57.

EXAMPLE 4   What is the smallest subdivision between the two integers 4 and 6?

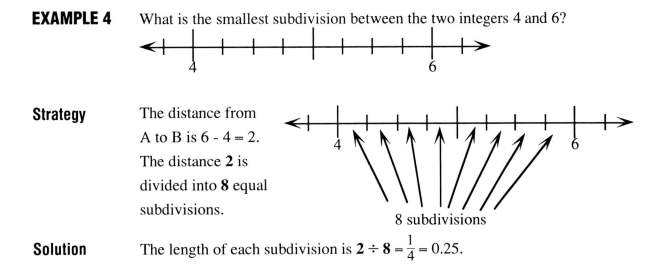

Strategy   The distance from A to B is 6 - 4 = 2. The distance **2** is divided into **8** equal subdivisions.

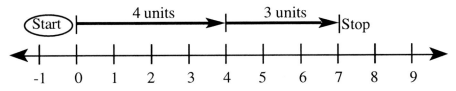

8 subdivisions

Solution   The length of each subdivision is $2 \div 8 = \frac{1}{4} = 0.25$.

You can use a number line to add numbers. For example, you can show the sum 4 + 3.

The addition is shown in terms of moves on a number line.

 Start at 0, move 4 units to the right (*positive direction*) to 4.

 Then move 3 more units to the right (*positive direction*) to 7.

So, 4 + 3 = 7.

This is read as **positive 4 plus positive 3 equals positive 7**.

EXAMPLE 5   Add -5 + (-3) using a number line.

Strategy   Start at 0.

 Move 5 units to the left (negative direction) to -5.

 Then move 3 more units to the left (negative direction) to -8.

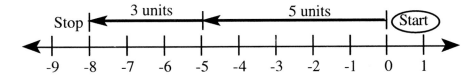

Solution   The sum is -8.

EXAMPLE 6   Add 5 + (-7) using a number line.

Strategy   Start at 0.

Move 5 units to the right (positive direction) to 5.

Then move 7 units to the left (negative direction) to -2.

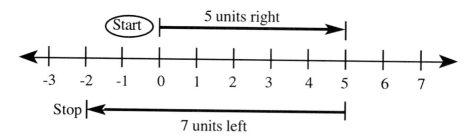

Solution   The sum is -2.

EXAMPLE 7   Add -8 + 9 using a number line.

Strategy   Start at 0.

Move 8 units to the left (negative) direction) to -8.

Then move 9 units to the right (positive direction) to 1.

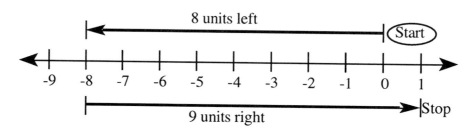

Solution   The sum is 1.

DISCOVERY   Find, on a calculator, the key marked **+/-** or **+ ↻ -** .

Enter 6   Enter +/-

What is the purpose of the **+/-** key?

How can you use this key to add -18 + 43?

EXAMPLE 8   Use a calculator to add -19 + (-49).

Enter 19	Enter +/-	Enter +	Enter 49	Enter +/-
Enter =	Read -68			

Solution   So, by calculator, -19 + (-49) = -68.

When adding several signed numbers without using a calculator, try to *imagine* movements to the left (**adding a negative number**) or to the right (**adding a positive number**).
This is illustrated in the next example.

EXAMPLE 9   The table at the right shows temperature changes for a cold winter day in Cody, Wyoming.
What is the temperature at midnight?

Time	Temperature	Change in Temperature
4:00 A.M	7°	
8:00 A.M.		dropped 9°
NOON		rose 4°
4:00 P.M.		rose 8°
8:00 P.M.		dropped 10°
Midnight	?°	dropped 8°

Strategy   Think in terms of movement on a number line.

Start at 7   **drop** 9   rise 4   rise 8   **drop** 10   **drop** 8

7   +   (-9)   +   4   +   8   +   (-10)   +   (-8)

Start at **7**, move **9 left** to -2.   **add -9**
From -2, move **4 right** to 2.   **add 4**
From 2, move **8 right** to 10.   **add 8**
From 10, move 10 **left** to 0.   **add -10**
From 2, move **8 left** to -8.   **add -8**

Solution   Thus, the temperature at midnight is -8°.

SUMMARY

1. How do you determine the proper inequality symbol to make -7 ? 4 a true statement?

2. How can you use the idea of temperature to insert the proper inequality symbol to make -3.486 ____ -3.485 a true statement?

3. How do you determine the smallest subdivision between the integers 5 and 8?

4. How do you use a calculator to simplify -29 + (-143)?

How do you use a number line to find each of the following sums?

5. -5 + (-3)   6. 5 + (-8)   7. -5 + 2   8. 9 + (-3)

SAMPLE EWT QUESTIONS

Insert the appropriate symbol to make each statement true: A. <   B. >   C. =

1. -8 ? 5   2. -8 ? -9   3. -8 ? -3   4. -8 ? 10

5. 4 ? -3   6. 7 ? -9   7. -3 ? 1   8. -6 ? $\boxed{2 + (-8)}$

Insert the appropriate inequality symbol to make each statement true.

9. -4.23 ____ -4.22   10. -7.13 ____ -7.14   11. -243.7 ____ -243.5

What is the smallest subdivision between the two integers?

12. A. $\frac{1}{2}$ B. $\frac{2}{3}$
    C. $1\frac{1}{2}$ D. 2

13. A. 0.25   B. 0.5
    C. 1   D. 4

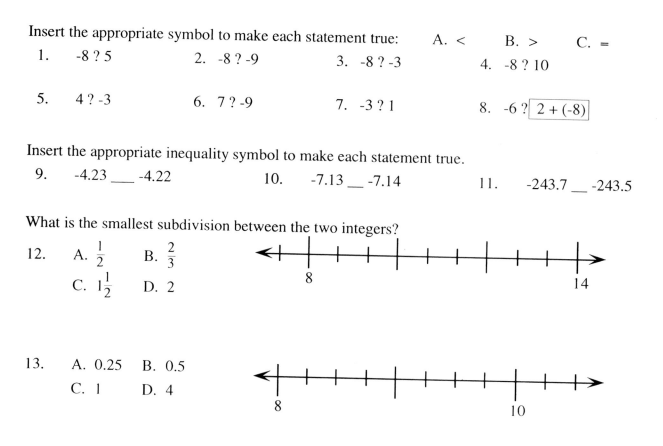

Add, using a number line.

14.	-7 + (-3)	15.	5 + (-8)	16.	-9 + 3	17.	-4 + (-2)
18.	-3 + (-4)	19.	-2 + (5)	20.	8 + (-9)	21.	-5 + (-7)

Add using a calculator.

22.   -143 + 219   23.   -719 + (-423)   24.   184 + (-731)

25.   Find the temperature at midnight.

Time	Temperature	Change in Temperature
500 A.M	6°	
7:00 A.M.		dropped 8°
NOON		rose 5°
3:00 P.M.		rose 2°
7:00 P.M.		dropped 7°
Midnight	?°	dropped 2°

26.   During a cold winter week the temperature fell 7°, rose 4°, fell 5°, and then rose 8°. If the temperature was 31° at the beginning of the week, what was it at the end of the five days?

OPEN-ENDED QUESTION

27.   You are playing a game in which you move a chip on a number line. Where you move the chip is determined by the cards you draw from a pack. Each card has an integer printed on it. Your chip is now at the location indicated below.

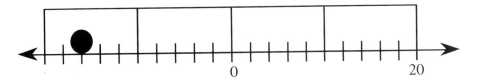

On each turn, you move your chip to the location with its coordinate equal to the sum of the coordinate of your current location and the integer on the card you draw.

(a)   Find the coordinate of the location of your chip now.

(b)   Suppose you got on your present location after 3 moves. What 3 integer cards might you have drawn?

REVIEW

1. Evaluate $x^2 + 5$ for $x = 3$.

   A. 45   B. 30   C. 14   D. 11

2. If x is a whole number less than 5 then 15 - x is

   A. < 0 B. > 0 but < 5 C. > 5 but < 10 D. > 10

3. What number has the following characteristics?

   * It is a prime number   * It is greater than 30

   * It is less than 40   * It does not have a 1 in the unit place.

   A. 31   B. 33   C. 37   D. none of these

4. Which of the following is not equal to the other three?

   A. $3 \cdot 3 + 1$ B. $\sqrt{49}$ C. $2^3 - 1$ D. $2 \cdot 3\frac{1}{2}$

5. A skirt that regularly sells for $40 is on sale at a discount of 20%.
   Which procedure below could you use to find the sale price?

   I $40 \cdot 0.20$ II $40 \cdot 1.20$

   III $40 - 0.20 \cdot 40$ IV $40 \cdot 0.80$

   A. I only   B. II only   C. III only   D. III or IV only

6. Mike mistakenly multiplied by 12 instead of dividing by 12 when using his calculator. If the incorrect answer displayed on the calculator is 72, what is the correct answer?

Use this table to answer Exercises 7-8.

Car	Cost (basic model)	Length	Weight
Oldsmobile 98	$23,240	212.4 inches	3,784 lb
Bonneville	$18,660	192.2 inches	3,119 lb
Caprice	$16,152	170.9 inches	2,344 lb
Cavalier	$13,024	189.9 inches	3,768 lb

7. Find the mean cost for the four models.

8. Identify the model with the following characteristics:

   cost more than $16,500

   length less than 200 in.

   weight between 2,500 lb and 3,500 lb

LESSON 9 PRE-ALGEBRA
Signed Numbers Part 2

The EWT guidelines do **NOT** call for formal knowledge of the rules for multiplying and dividing signed numbers.

However, you will have to know how to multiply a positive number times a negative number.

Remember from arithmetic that 2 times 3 means 3 + 3:   **add two threes**.

So, 4 · 5 means 5 + 5 + 5 + 5:   **add four fives**.

Similarly, 4 · -5 means $\boxed{-5 + (-5) + (-5) + (-5)}$: **add four negative fives**.

$$\downarrow$$

-20

(Start at 0: move 5 to the left to -5, then 5 more to the left to -10, then 5 more to the left to -15, and finally 5 more to the left to -20.)

Similarly,

$$7 \cdot -3 = -21$$
$$8 \cdot -6 = -48$$
$$-4 \cdot 9 = 9 \cdot -4 = -36$$

Multiplication can be done in any order.

This suggests a rule, the only one for signed numbers that you will need for the EWT.

The product of a negative number and positive number is a negative number.

EXAMPLE 1   Multiply: 8 · -5.

Solution   8 · -5 = -40   **pos.· neg. = neg.**

To evaluate 2x + 5 for x = -6 involves **both** multiplication and addition.

$$2x \quad + 5$$
$$2 \cdot \textbf{-6} + 5 \qquad \text{\textbf{Replace x by -6.}}$$
$$-12 \; + 5 \qquad \text{\textbf{Multiply first:} \quad pos.· neg. = neg.}$$
$$-7 \qquad \text{\textbf{Add, using a number line.}}$$

-75-

Subtraction can be thought of in terms of adding signed numbers.

For example: $\boxed{8 - 3}$ $\boxed{12 - 7}$

$\downarrow$ $\downarrow$

$8 + (-3)$ $12 + (-7)$

EXAMPLE 2   Evaluate 4a - 3 for a = -2.

Strategy
4a -3	
4 · -2 -3	**Replace a by -2.**
-8 -3	**Multiply first: pos.· neg. = neg.**
-8 + (-3)	**Rewrite as addition.**

Solution   -11   **Add using a number line.**

EXAMPLE 3   Which of these groups of numbers

correctly completes this table as y values for x?

A. 0 and -5   B. 4 and -13

B. 4 and -2   D. 4 and -5

$y = 3x + 4$		
x	3x + 4	y
2	3(2) + 4	10
1	3(1) + 4	7
0		
-3		

Strategy   Evaluate 3x + 4 for x = 0 and x = -3.

3x + 4 for x = 0   3x + 4 for x = -3

3 · 0 + 4   3 · -3 + 4

0 + 4   -9 + 4   **Multiply first.**

4   -5   **Add using a number line.**

Solution   Thus, the y values are 4 and -5, Choice D.

EXAMPLE 4   A group of students reviewed for a science test by playing a game.

Three points were allowed for each correct answer.

But two points were lost for each wrong one.

If one student gave 2 correct answers and 4 wrong answers to the first six

questions, what would that student's score be? (Negative scores were possible.)

Strategy   Write an expression for the total score.

(continued on next page)

Total score is   number correct · 3   +   number wrong · **-2 (points lost)**

Total score is $\boxed{2}$ · 3   + $\boxed{4}$ · **-2**

                          6   +   -8

                                  -2

Solution   Thus, the student's score was -2.

EXAMPLE 5   What point pictured on this number line represents the product of $-\frac{1}{2}$ and 3?

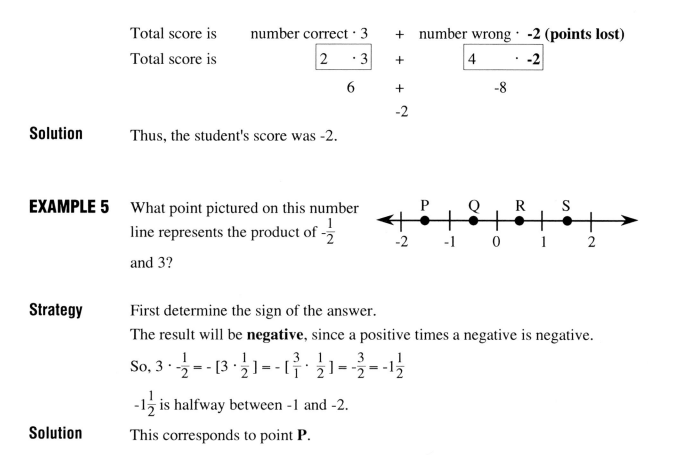

Strategy   First determine the sign of the answer.

The result will be **negative**, since a positive times a negative is negative.

So, $3 \cdot -\frac{1}{2} = -[3 \cdot \frac{1}{2}] = -[\frac{3}{1} \cdot \frac{1}{2}] = -\frac{3}{2} = -1\frac{1}{2}$

$-1\frac{1}{2}$ is halfway between -1 and -2.

Solution   This corresponds to point **P**.

SUMMARY

1.   What is the sign of the product 49 · -19?
2.   How do you evaluate 3a + 5 for a = -4?
3.   How can 5x - 4 be written as addition?
4.   How do you evaluate 5x - 4 for x = -2?

SAMPLE EWT QUESTIONS

1.   -4 · 6 = ?

    A. 24   B. 2   C. -10   D. -24

Evaluate each for the given value of the variable.

2.   2x + 5 for x = -3   3. 5x + 12 for x = -2

    A. -30   B. -1   A. 2   B. 15

    C. 4   D. 11   C. -2   D. -120

4. 3a + 1 for a = -4

    A. -11   B. -13

    C. 0   D. 13

5. 5x + 3 for x = -2

    A. 13   B. 7

    C. -7   D. -13

6. 3b - 4 for b = -2

    A. -10   B. -3

    C. 2   D. 10

7. 4y - 5 for y = -1

    A. -1   B. -2

    C. -8   D. -9

8. -2m + 6 for m = 3

    A. -12   B. 0

    C. 7   D. 12

9. -5a - 4 for a = 2

    A. 6   B. -6

    C. -7   D. -14

Which group of numbers correctly completes each table as y values for x?

10.

$y = 2x + 5$

x	2x + 5	y
2	2(2) + 5	9
1	2(1) + 5	7
0		
-3		

    A. 0 and -1   B. 5 and -1

    C. 5 and -30   D. 5 and 4

11.

$y = 3x - 1$

x	3x - 1	y
2	3(2) - 1	5
1	3(1) - 1	2
-1		
-3		

    A. -4 and -10   B. 2 and 8

    C. -5 and -1   D. 4 and 10

12. The scoring rules for a quiz game are four points for each correct answer and three points lost for each wrong answer. If one player gave 2 correct answers and 3 wrong answers to the first five questions, what would that player's score be?

13. A group of students reviewed for a science test by playing a game.

    Four points were allowed for each correct answer.

    Two points were lost for each wrong one.

If one student gave 2 correct answers and 5 wrong answers to the first seven questions, what would that student's score be?. (Negative scores were possible.)

14. What point pictured on this number line represents the product of $-\frac{1}{2}$ and 5?

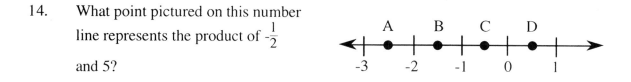

15. What point pictured on this number line represents the product of 7 and $-\frac{1}{4}$?

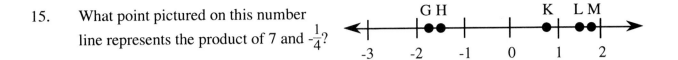

Evaluate each for the given value of the variable.

16. 7x - 4 for x = -2

17. 9 + 3x for x = -5

18. -3m + 7 for m = 2

19. -5 + 8t for t = -2

OPEN-ENDED QUESTION

20. Examine the pattern below.

Complete the pattern and use it to write the rule for multiplying signed numbers with the **same** sign, such as -5 · -3 and 4 · 8.

The pattern uses what you have just learned: (-) · (+) = (-).

-3 · 3 = -9

-3 · 2 = -6

-3 · 1 = -3   **(The product increases by 3 each time.)**

-3 · 0 = 0

-3 · -1 = ?

-3 · -2 = ?

-3 · -3 = ?

REVIEW

1. Nigel has an appointment for a job interview exactly three weeks from today. Today is April 28. On what date is his interview?

   A. April 5   B. May 4

   C. May 5   D. May 19

APRIL						
Sun	Mon	Tues	Wed	Thur	Fri	Sat
			1	2	3	4
5	6	7	8	9	10	11
12	13	14	15	16	17	18
19	20	21	22	23	24	25
26	27	28	29	30		

Add, using a number line.

2. -5 + 8

   A. 13   B. 3

   C. -3   D. -13

3. -7 + (-5)

   A. -12   B. -2

   C. 2   D. 12

4. Find 17 less than 39.

   A.   46   B. 56   C. 22   D. 663

5. Round each price to the nearest dollar. Estimate the change due back from paying with a $20 bill.

   A. $2   B. $4

   C. $16   D. $18

   Jersey Shore Grocery
   $ 6.23
   $ 2.99
   $ 2.62
   $ 0.79
   $ 1.35
   $ 0.83
   $ 1.04
   $ 0.35
   $ 0.49
   _____ TOTAL

6. Tanya is shopping for magic markers and wants the lowest price per marker. What choice will give her what she wants?

   A. 4 for $2.39   B. 1 dozen for $6.00

   C. 3 for $2.25   D. 2 dozen for $11.76

7. Which of these is the closest approximation of $\sqrt{5000}$?

   A. 250   B. 71   C. 68   D. 25

8. The eighth graders in one school collected toys for needy children. This year 150 students gave toys. This figure is 80% of what it was last year. This means that

   A. 80 more students gave toys this year than last year.

   B. the number of students giving toys decreased from last year to this year.

   C. 120 students gave toys last year.

   D. the number of students giving toys increased from last year to this year.

9. A music store sells popular cassette tapes at a rate of 3 for $25.30 and blank cassette tapes at a rate of $9.38 a dozen. Assume that the store manager requires rounding up to the nearest cent. Find the total cost, without sales tax, for two popular tapes and one blank tape.

10. Video Special Buys is selling a video game at $\frac{1}{4}$ off its regular price of $64. The same game is selling for 30% off its regular price of $70 at Games Galore. How much is saved by buying the game at the store with the best buy?

LESSON 10 PRE-ALGEBRA
Equations

In this lesson you will review solving equations.

To solve an equation like x - 4 = 8, you try to get an equivalent equation with x alone on one side of the equals symbol.

Remember that you can **add** the same number to, or **subtract** the same number from, each side of an equation.

EXAMPLE 1   Solve x - 7 = 9

Strategy   x is on the left side of the equals symbol.

7 is being subtracted from x.

To **undo** subtraction of 7, **ADD** 7 to each side of the equation.

x - 7	= 9	
x - 7 + 7	= 9 + 7	**Add 7 to each side.**
x + 0	= 16	**-7 + 7 = 0**
Solution x	= 16	**x + 0 = x**

EXAMPLE 2   Solve 12 = a + 8

Strategy   **a** is on the right side of the equals symbol.

8 is being added to a.

To **undo** addition of 8, **SUBTRACT** 8 from each side of the equation.

12	= a + 8	
12 - 8	= a + 8 - 8	**Subtract 8 from each side.**
Solution 4	= a + 0	
4	= a	**a + 0 = a**

You can **multiply** each side of an equation by the same number.

You can **divide** each side of an equation by the same non-zero number.

EXAMPLE 3   Solve $3m = 15$

Strategy   **m** is being multiplied by 3.

To **undo** multiplication by 3, **DIVIDE** each side of the equation by 3.

$$3m = 15$$

$$\frac{3m}{3} = \frac{15}{3}$$ **Divide each side by 3.**

$$1m = 5$$

Solution $m = 5$

$$\frac{3m}{3} = \frac{3 \cdot m}{3} = \frac{1\cancel{3} \cdot m}{\cancel{3}_1} = 1m = m$$

EXAMPLE 4   Solve $\frac{x}{5} = 6$.

Strategy   **x** is not alone on the left of the equals symbol because x is **divided** by 5

To **undo** division by 5, **MULTIPLY** each side of the equation by 5.

$$\frac{x}{5} = 6$$

$$5 \cdot \frac{x}{5} = 5 \cdot 6$$ **Multiply each side by 5.**

$$1x = 30$$

Solution $x = 30$

$$5 \cdot \frac{x}{5} = 1\cancel{5} \cdot \frac{x}{\cancel{5}_1} = 1x = x$$

Sometimes **two undoings** are needed to solve an equation.

This is illustrated in the next two Examples.

EXAMPLE 5   Solve $\frac{3k}{4} = 9$.

Strategy   First, k is multiplied by 3, and then divided by 4.

(continued on next page)

$$\frac{3k}{4} = 9$$

$$4 \cdot \frac{3k}{4} = 4 \cdot 9 \qquad \textbf{UNDO division by 4. Multiply each side by 4.}$$

$$3k = 36$$

$$\frac{3k}{3} = \frac{36}{3} \qquad \textbf{UNDO multiplication by 3. Divide each side by 3.}$$

$$1k = 12$$

Solution $\qquad k = 12$

To solve the equation $x + 7 = 12$ you have to **undo one** operation, **addition**.

To solve the equation $3x = 30$ you have to **undo one** operation, **multiplication**.

Consider the equation $3x + 7 = 22$.

How many operations do you think will have to be **undone**?

EXAMPLE 6   Solve $4x + 20 = 80$.

Strategy $\qquad 4x + 20 = 80 \qquad$ **To undo addition of 20,**

$$4x + 20 - 20 = 80 - 20 \qquad \textbf{subtract 20 from each side.}$$

$$4x + 0 = 60$$

$$4x = 60 \qquad \textbf{To undo multiplication by 4,}$$

$$\frac{4x}{4} = \frac{60}{4} \qquad \textbf{divide each side by 4, NOT -4.}$$

$$1x = 15$$

Solution $\qquad x = 15$

EXAMPLE 7   Solve $21 = 15 + 3a$.

Strategy $\qquad 21 = 15 \quad + 3a \qquad$ **3a is not alone on the right: 15 is**
$\qquad\qquad\qquad\qquad\qquad\qquad\qquad\quad$ **added to 3a. Undo addition of 15.**

$$21 - 15 = 15 - 15 \quad + 3a \qquad \textbf{Subtract 15 from each side.}$$

$$6 = 0 \quad + 3a$$

$$6 = 3a$$

$$\frac{6}{3} = \frac{3a}{3} \qquad \textbf{To undo multiplication by 3,}$$

$$2 = 1a \qquad \textbf{divide each side by 3.}$$

Solution $\qquad 2 = a$

SUMMARY

1. To solve $5x = 35$, what operation must be undone? What must you do to each side of the equation?

2. To solve $\frac{a}{4} = 7$, what operation must be undone? What must you do to each side of the equation?

3. To solve $\frac{5b}{4} = 15$, first _____ each side of the equation by _____.

    Then _____ each side of the resulting equation by _____.

To solve the equation $3y - 6 = 24$—

4. What two operations must be undone?

5. What operation must be undone first?

6. How is this done?

7. What is the resulting equation?

8. What operation must now be undone?

9. How is this done?

10. What is the solution?

SAMPLE EWT QUESTIONS

Solve each equation. (Exercises 1-12)

1. $x - 4 = 9$

    A. $\frac{9}{4}$ B. 5

    C. 13   D. 36

2. $a + 5 = 13$

    A. $\frac{13}{5}$ B. 8

    C. 21   D. 65

3. $11 = 7 + a$

    A. $\frac{11}{4}$ B. 14

    C. 4   D. 44

4. $7x = 28$

    A. 4   B. 21

    C. 35   D. 112

5. $24 = 6b$

    A. 144   B. 30

    C. 18   D. 4

6. $5t = 45$

    A. 50   B. 40

    C. 225   D. 9

7. $\frac{Y}{3} = 6$

    A. 2   B. 3

    C. 9   D. 18

8. $14 = \frac{m}{2}$

    A. 28   B. 16

    C. 12   D. 7

9. $\frac{p}{5} = 10$

    A. 2   B. 15

    C. 50   D. 5

10. $3x - 2 = 13$

   A. $\frac{11}{3}$ B. 5

   C. 8   D. 13

11. $9 = 10t + 5$

   A. $\frac{2}{5}$ B. $\frac{7}{5}$

   C. 5   D. 6

12. $49 = 9e + 4$

   A. 4.5   B. 5

   C. 7   D. 10

13. For the equation $-384x = 375$, which of the following statements is true about the correct value of x?

   A. The value of x is negative.

   B. The value of x is positive

   C. The value of x is zero

   D. It is not possible to tell if the value of x is negative, positive, or zero.

Solve each equation.

14. $10x - 7 = 18$

15. $24 = 6 + 3x$

16. $32 = 4n - 8$

17. $4a + 5 = 13$

18. $23 = 7 + 5c$

19. $14 = 2x - 18$

20. $356v - 194 = 234$

21. $1,456 = 17.3m + 987$

OPEN-ENDED QUESTION

22. Explain how to solve an equation like $4x - 8 = 32$. For each step in the solution, explain how you know what to do to each side of the equation.

REVIEW

1. Evaluate $4x + 2$ for $x = -3$

   A. -24   B. -10   C. 3   D. 14

2. Insert the appropriate inequality symbol to make -5.28 ? -5.27 true.

   A. <   B. >   C. =   D. You can't tell.

Add using a number line.

3. $-6 + (-8)$

4. $-9 + 5$

5. $12 + (-15)$

6. What digit is in the 35th decimal place when $\frac{5}{7}$ is written as a decimal?

LESSON 11 PRE-ALGEBRA
Equations, Distributive Property, Like Terms

An expression like $4x + 5 + 2x$ has three terms: $4x$, 5, and $2x$.

The terms $4x$ and $2x$ are **like** terms. (They both contain the variable x.)

The expression $4x + 5 + 2x$ can be simplified by **combining like terms**.

$4x + 5 + 2x$	$=$	$\boxed{4x + 2x} + 5$	**Group like terms together.**
	$=$	$6x + 5$	**Combine like terms.**

$4a - 2 + a$	$=$	$\boxed{4a + a} - 2$	**Group like terms together.**
	$=$	$4a + 1a - 2$	**Rewrite a as 1a.**
	$=$	$5a - 2$	**Combine like terms.**

Sometimes an equation contains like terms on the same side of the equation.

In this case, first **combine like terms**.

Then solve the resulting equation.

EXAMPLE 1 Solve $3n - 2 + n = 14$

Strategy On the left side of the = symbol there are two like terms, **3n** and **n**.

$\mathbf{3n - 2 + n}$ $= 14$		
$\mathbf{3n + n} - 2$ $= 14$	**Group like terms together.**	
$\boxed{3n + 1n} + 2 = 14$	**n = 1n.**	
$4n + 2$ $= 14$	**Combine like terms.**	
$4n + 2 - \mathbf{2} = 14 - \mathbf{2}$	**Subtract 2 from each side.**	
$4n + 0$ $= 12$		
$4n$ $= 12$		
$\dfrac{4n}{4}$ $= \dfrac{12}{4}$		

Solution $n = 3$

Sometimes the **Distributive Property** is needed to solve an equation.

Let's review how to apply the **Distributive Property**.

EXAMPLE 2   Simplify 4(3y - 2).

Strategy	4(3y - 2)	=	$4 \cdot 3y - 4 \cdot 2$	**Distribute 4 to both 3y and 2.**
Solution		=	12y - 8	**Think: $4 \cdot 3y = 4 \cdot 3 \cdot y$**
				= 12y

The equation 7 + 2(5x + 2) = 31 contains parentheses.

In this case, use the Distributive Property to remove parentheses.

Combine like terms.

Solve the resulting equation.

This is illustrated in the next example.

EXAMPLE 3   Solve 7 + 2(5x + 2) = 31.

Strategy	7 + 2(5x + 2)	= 31	
	$7 + 2 \cdot 5x + 2 \cdot 2$	= 31	**Apply the Distributive Property.**
	7 + 10x + 4	= 31	
	10x + 11	= 31	**Combine like terms: 7 + 4 = 11.**
	10x + 11 - **11**	= 31 - **11**	**Subtract 11 from each side.**
	10x + 0	= 20	
	10x	= 20	
	$\dfrac{10x}{10}$	$= \dfrac{20}{10}$	**Divide each side by 10.**
Solution	x	= 2	

You need not write out all the steps in Example 3.

You can shorten your work as follows.

	7 + 2(5x + 2)	= 31	
	$7 + 2 \cdot 5x + 2 \cdot 2$	= 31	**Apply the Distributive Property.**
	7 + 10x + 4	= 31	
	10x + 11	= 31	**Combine like terms: 7 + 4 = 11.**
	10x	= 20	**Subtract 11 from each side.**
	x	= 2	**Divide each side by 10.**

You have already worked with **data tables**. Sometimes equations with parentheses are used in connection with a data table. This is illustrated in Example 4 below.

EXAMPLE 4 Complete the data table at the right.

m	m + 3(2m - 4)
5	
	2

Strategy **Step 1** To complete the first row, **evaluate** m + 3(2m - 4) for **m = 5**.

$m + 3(2m - 4)$

$5 + 3(2 \cdot 5 - 4)$ **Substitute 5 for m.**

$5 + 3(10 - 4)$

$5 + 3 \quad (6)$

$5 + 18$

23

Step 2 To complete the second row, find m.

Solve the equation m + 3(2m - 4) = 2.

$1m + 3(2m - 4)$	$= 2$	**m = 1m**
$1m + 3 \cdot 2m - 3 \cdot 4$	$= 2$	**Distribute the 3.**
$1m + 6m - 12$	$= 2$	
$7m - 12$	$= 2$	**Combine like terms.**
$7m$	$= 14$	**Add 12 to each side.**
m	$= 2$	**Divide each side by 7.**

Solution Thus, the completed table is:

m	m + 3(2m - 4)
5	23
m = 2 → 2	2

EXAMPLE 5 If x is the same in both of the equations below, what is y?

$2(x + 4) = 14$

$x + y = 11$

Strategy Solve the first equation for x.

Then substitute this value of x in the **second** equation.

Solve the resulting equation for y.

(continued on next page)

Step 1   Solve the first equation for x.

$2(x + 4)$ $= 14$

$2 \cdot x + 2 \cdot 4$ $= 14$ **Apply the Distributive Property.**

$2x + 8$ $= 14$

$2x$ $= 6$ **Subtract 8 from each side.**

x $= 3$ **Divide each side by 2.**

Step 2   Substitute **3** for **x** in the second equation.

$x + y = 11$
↓

$3 + y = 11$

Step 3   Solve $3 + y = 11$ for y.

$y = 8$ **Subtract 3 from each side.**

Solution   Thus, $y = 8$.

Example 6   All cylinders have identical weights. All boxes have identical weights. The weight of 3 cylinders is the same as the weight of 1 box.

Side A

Side B

The scales will be balanced after adding which one of the following to side B?

A. 4 cylinders

B. 1 box and 2 cylinders

C. 5 cylinders

D. 2 boxes

Strategy   The weight of 3 cylinders is the same as the weight of 1 box.

Imagine replacing each box by 3 cylinders.

How many cylinders will then be on the left side of the scale?

How many cylinders will then be on the right side of the scale?

How many more cylinders will be needed on the right side to balance the scale?

(continued on next page)

Below is a sketch showing the result of replacing each box by 3 cylinders.

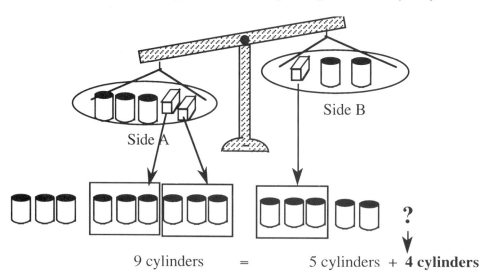

9 cylinders   =   5 cylinders + **4 cylinders**

Thus, you need to add **4 cylinders** to side B to balance the scale.

Solution   The correct choice is **A.**

EXAMPLE 7   All objects with the same shape have equal weights.
The weight of 1 box is the same as the weight of 2 cylinders.
The weight of 1 cylinder is the same as the weight of 2 pyramids. Which of these actions would balance the scale?

I   Add 1 pyramid to Side B.

II   Remove 1 cylinder from Side A

III   Add 1 pyramid to side A and add 1 cylinder to Side B.

IV   Remove 1 pyramid from Side B.

A. I or III only   B. II or IV only

C. I only   D. IV only

Strategy   Sometimes the easiest way to solve a problem with many choices is to check each choice one at a time to see which ones work.

(continued on next page)

Check Action I first.

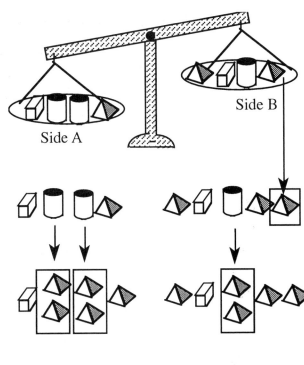

Add 1 pyramid to Side B.

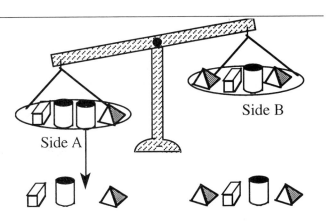

Then use 1 cylinder equals 2 pyramids. Each side now contains 5 pyramids and 1 block.

Thus, Action I balances the scale.

Check Action II next.

Remove 1 cylinder from Side A. The two sides are **NOT** balanced. There is an extra pyramid on Side B.

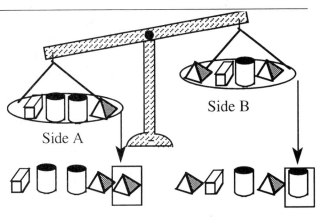

Check Action III.

Add 1 pyramid to side A, 1 cylinder to Side B. The sides are balanced. Each side contains 2 cylinders, 2 pyramids, and 1 block.

Thus, Action III also balances the scale.

(continued on next page)

-91-

Finally, let's check Action IV

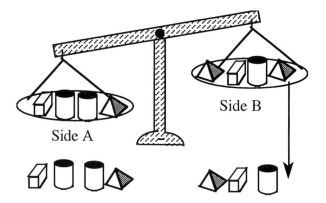

Side A

Side B

Remove 1 pyramid from Side B.
The two sides are **NOT** balanced. There is an extra cylinder on Side A.

Solution   So, Actions I or III balance the scale.
The correct choice is therefore A.

EXAMPLE 8   What is the weight of one of the blocks if each pyramid weighs 2 pounds and the scale is balanced?

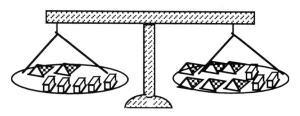

Strategy   Think of this problem as solving an equation.

First take away as many pyramids as you can from each side of the balance scale.

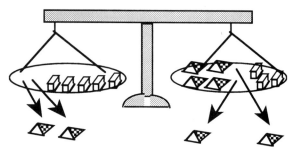

Take away **2 pyramids** from each side.

Now take away as many blocks as you can from each side.
You don't have to draw all of these diagrams. Think the process in your head.

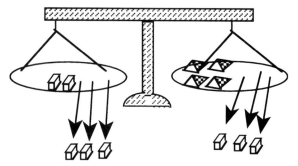

Take away **3 blocks** from each side.

The scale is left with **2** blocks on the left and **4** pyramids on the right.

Let x = the weight of each block.   The weight of each pyramid is 2 lb.

balanced

x   x   2   2   2   2

Write an equation.	$2x$	$= 8$
Solve the equation.	$\dfrac{2x}{2}$	$= \dfrac{8}{2}$ **Divide each side by 2.**

Solution x $= 4$

Thus, the weight of each block is 4 lb.

SUMMARY

1.   How do you simplify $3a + 5 + 2a$?

2.   How do you think of rewriting x in $7x + x$ when combining like terms?

3.   How do use the Distributive Property to simplify $3(2b + 4)$?

Use the equation $5 + 3(2x + 4) = 41$ to answer Exercises 4-6.

4.   What is the first step in solving this equation? What is the result?

5.   It is now necessary to _____ ____ _____. What is the result?

6.   Solve the resulting equations.

7.   How do you find the missing value in the first row?

8.   How do you find the missing value in the second row?

x	x + 2(3x - 2)
4	
	10

9.   x has the same value in both equations below.

$2(x - 5) = 8$ $2x + 3y = 21$

What is the first step in finding y? What is the second step?

10.   The weight of 2 cylinders is the same as the weight of 1 box. How can you find the number of cylinders that must be added to Side B to balance the scale?

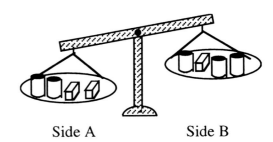

Side A   Side B

SAMPLE EWT QUESTIONS

Solve each equation.

1. $4x + 8 + x = 28$ 2. $6b - 4 + b = 45$ 3. $52 = y + 24 + 3y$

4. $4(x - 2) = 36$ 5. $6(4 + x) = 66$ 6. $16 = 8(a - 4)$

7. $3x + 2(4x + 1) = 35$ 8. $3a + 5(4a - 1) = 41$

9. $4a + 2(3a + 1) = 32$ 10. $6x + 4(3x - 5) = 16$

11. $3x + 7 + x = 23$

   A. 2.1   B. 4

   C. 7.5   D. 10

12. $42 = m + 24 + 5m$

   A. 11   B. 3.6

   C. 3   D. 2

13. $4x + 2(3x + 2) = 34$

   A. 3   B. 3.1

   C. 3.2   D. 3.8

14. $2a + 3(2a + 5) = 31$

   A. 5.75   B. 3.25

   C. 2.29   D. 2

If x is the same number in both of the equations below, what is y?

15. $3 + x = 7$

   $x + y = 9$

   A. 2   B. 3

   C. 5   D. 6

If x is the same number in both of the equations below, what is y?

16. $2x - 4 = 12$

   $3x + 2y = 30$

   A. 3   B. 8

   C. 9   D. 27

17. Which of these groups of numbers correctly completes this table?

   A. 7 and 3.5   B. 13 and 3

   C. 13 and 1.3   D. 10 and 3

x	x + 3(2x - 5)
4	
	6

18. Which of these groups of numbers correctly completes this table?

   A. -11 and 28   B. -11 and 34

   C. 31 and 34   D. -31 and 28

n	7(n - 8) + 2n
5	
	196

19. Find the weight of one pyramid if one block weighs 4 lb and the scale is balanced.

    A. $\frac{2}{3}$ lb   B. 1 lb

    C. $\frac{8}{3}$ lb   D. 3 lb

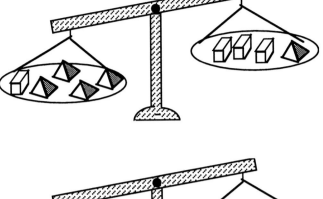

20. All objects with the same shape have equal weights.
    The weight of 1 box is the same as the weight of 3 cylinders.
    The weight of 1 cylinder is the same as the weight of 2 pyramids. Which of these actions would balance the scale?

    I   Add 1 pyramid to side B.

    II   Add 1 pyramid to side A.

    III Add 1 pyramid to side B and add 1 cylinder to side A.

    IV   Remove 1 pyramid from side B.

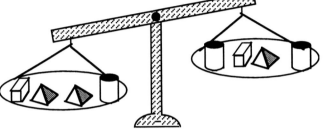

Side A   Side B

    A. I or III only
    B. II, III, or IV only
    C. II only
    D. III only

21. All objects with the same shape have equal weights. Two boxes have the same weight as one cylinder. The scales will be balanced after adding which of the following to side B?
    A. 1 cylinder and 1 box
    B. 2 boxes
    C. 2 boxes and 1 cylinder
    D. 1 box

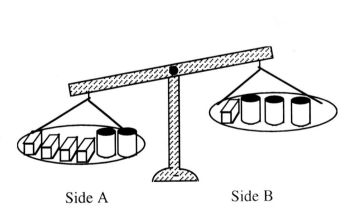

Side A   Side B

OPEN-ENDED QUESTION

22. Suppose the weight of one pyramid is the same as the weight of 4 blocks. How many blocks or pyramids or combinations of blocks and pyramids can you add to which side (left or right) to balance the scales?

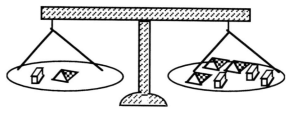

Is there more than one answer?

Explain how you got your answer.

REVIEW

1. Suppose that $\frac{x}{4} > 20$. Which of the following statements is true?

    A. x is less than 4.

    B. x is between 4 and 20.

    C. x is greater than 80.

    D. x is between 20 and 80

    HINT: Try each multiple-choice item.

2. Use this table to answer the question below.

Mail Subscription Rates	1 mo.	3 mos.	6 mos.	1 year
Weekdays and Sundays	$17.35	$50.25	$97.50	$185.00
Weekdays	$12.45	$36.95	$72.00	$141.00
Sundays	$4.45	$12.85	$26.25	$48.00

    How much would be saved by ordering a one-year subscription to the Gazette News for weekdays at the special one-year subscription rate compared to the monthly rate for the same type of subscription?

    A. $149.40   B. $128.55   C. $23.20   D. $8.40

3. Insert two fractions between $\frac{1}{2}$ and $\frac{4}{5}$.

4. Every fifteen minutes the number of bacteria in a science experiment approximately doubles. The population at 4 P.M. was about one-quarter of a million bacteria. Find the approximate size of the population at 4:45 P.M.

LESSON 12   PRE-ALGEBRA
Word Problems

Consider the phrase **6 increased by a number**.

The number might be -4, 2, 0, or any number.

If you let a letter or variable represent the number, say **n**, then

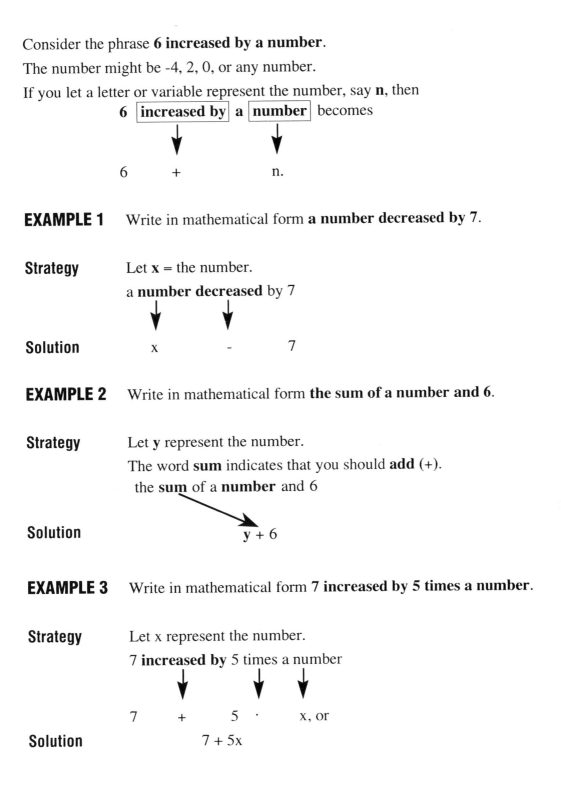

EXAMPLE 1   Write in mathematical form **a number decreased by 7**.

Strategy   Let **x** = the number.

a number decreased by 7

Solution   x   -   7

EXAMPLE 2   Write in mathematical form **the sum of a number and 6**.

Strategy   Let **y** represent the number.

The word **sum** indicates that you should **add** (+).

the **sum** of a **number** and 6

Solution   **y + 6**

EXAMPLE 3   Write in mathematical form **7 increased by 5 times a number**.

Strategy   Let x represent the number.

7 increased by 5 times a number

7   +   5   ·   x, or

Solution   7 + 5x

Another frequently used expression is **less than**.

For example, 6 less than 13 does **NOT** mean 6 - 13.

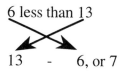

6 less than 13

13 - 6, or 7

Note the **switching** of the order of subtraction for the phrase **less than**.

Similarly, there is the phrase **more than**.

8 more than 3 means 3 made greater by 8.

3 + 8, or 11

EXAMPLE 4   Write in mathematical form **7 less than twice Harry's age**.

Strategy   Let **A** represent Harry's Age.

7 less than twice Harry's **Age**

7 less than **2 · Harry's Age**

7 less than **2 · A**

7 less than 2A

Solution   2A - 7

EXAMPLE 5   Which problem below can be solved by the equation x + 6 = 40?

A. Maria was paid $40 for this week's part-ime work as a maid. She received a $6.00 tip. How much money did she then have?

B. Bert biked 40 miles at 6 miles per hour. How long did he bike?

C. Ron added 6 more stamps to his stamp collection. If he now has 40 stamps in his collection, how many did he have before adding six more?

D. By noon, a motel had 40 guests registered. Six more guests registered by 6:00 P.M. How many guests were then registered?

(continued on next page)

Strategy   You will have to check the equation for each multiple-choice item
to see which one matches x + 6 = 40.

Choice A   salary + tip = total
40 + 6 = x   **(NOT x + 6 =40)**

Choice B.   To find distance biked, use this method:
mph times number of h. is miles biked
For example, 6 mph for 2 h is 6 · 2 = 12 miles.
mph times number of h. is miles biked
6 · x = 40   **(NOT x + 6= 40)**

Choice C.   original + 6 new ones is total 40.
x + 6 = 40   **CHOICE C!**

Solution   You don't need to check Choice D. You have found that **C** is correct.

EXAMPLE 6   9 less than 3 times Fantashia's age is 33.
How old is Fantashia?

Strategy   You are asked to find Fantashia's age.
Let F = Fantashia's age.   **Use a letter to represent
what you are asked to find.**

Use the first sentence to write an equation.

9 less than 3 times **F**antashia's age is 33.
9 less than 3 times **F** is 33
9 less than 3 · F is 33
9 less than 3F is 33

Solve: 3F - 9 = 33

3F = 42   **Add 9 to each side.**

F = 14   **Divide each side by 3.**

Solution   Thus, Fantashia's age is 14.

EXAMPLE 7   The $340 selling price of a stereo is $40 more than 3 times the cost. Find the cost of the stereo.

Strategy   You are asked to find the Cost of the stereo.

Let **C** = the Cost of the stereo.   **Use a letter to represent what you are asked to find.**

Use the first sentence to **write an equation**.

340 is 40 more than 3 times Cost
340 is 40 more than 3C

340 = 3C   +   40

Solve   340 = 3C + 40.

300 = 3C   **Subtract 40 from each side.**

100 =   C   **Divide each side by 100.**

Solution   Thus, the cost of the stereo is $100.

EXAMPLE 8   Write an equation you could use to solve the following word problem:
The sum of 14 and twice a number is 45.
Find the number.

Strategy   You are asked to find the number.

Let x = the number   **Use a letter to represent what you are asked to find.**

Use the first sentence to write an equation.

sum of 14 and twice a number is 45

Solution   14 +   2x   = 45

Recall how to find the average of four test grades 100, 80, 88, and 92.

If you let **A** represent the **average**, the formula is: $A = \dfrac{100 + 80 + 88 + 92}{4} = 90$.

Some applications of **average** involve solving algebraic equations.

This is illustrated in the next two examples.

EXAMPLE 9   John wants to have an average 90 on his math test scores.

His test grades so far are 75, 85, and 100. What must he get on the fourth test so that his average for the four tests will be 90?

Strategy   Let x be the grade he needs on the next test.

Write a formula for the average of his four test grades: 75, 85, 100, **x**.

$$\frac{\text{sum of test scores}}{\text{number of tests}} = \frac{75 + 85 + 100 + x}{4} = 90$$

Solve: $\dfrac{75 + 85 + 100 + x}{4} = 90$

$\dfrac{260 + x}{4} = 90$ **Combine like terms.**

$4 \cdot \dfrac{260 + x}{4} = 4 \cdot 90$ **Multiply each side by 4.**

$260 + x = 360$

$x = 100$ **Subtract 260 from each side.**

Solution   Thus, John must get 100 on the next test.

EXAMPLE 10   This semester Jane's math test average for four tests is exactly 89.

What must she get on the her fifth test to have an average of exactly 90?

Strategy   Even though she might have different scores on each test so far, the average for all four is 89. Therefore, let's assume that each score was 89 when writing an equation to solve the problem.

Let x be the grade she needs on the fifth test.

Write the formula for the average of five test grades: 89, 89, 89, 89, x.

$$\frac{\text{sum of data}}{\text{number of tests}} = \frac{89 + 89 + 89 + 89 + x}{5} = 90$$

Solve: $\dfrac{89 + 89 + 89 + 89 + x}{5} = 90$

$\dfrac{356 + x}{5} = 90$ **Combine like terms.**

$5 \cdot \dfrac{356 + x}{5} = 5 \cdot 90$ **Multiply each side by 5.**

$356 + x = 450$

$x = 94$ **Subtract 356 from each side.**

Solution   Thus, Jane must get **94** on her last test.

SUMMARY

How do you write each of the following in mathematical form?

1. a number decreased by 7

2. the sum of a number and 5

3. 4 increased by twice a number

4. 8 less than 3 times a number

Use the following problem to answer Exercises 5-9.

9 less than 3 times a number is 33. Find the number.

5. The first step is to use a letter or variable to represent _____.

6. Use this variable to next write an _____.

7. How do you write 9 less than 3 times n?

8. What is the equation?

9. What are the steps in solving this equation?

10. Bill has three test scores of 80, 90, and 90. How do you find the score he needs on the fourth and last test to achieve an average of 90?

SAMPLE EWT QUESTIONS

1. Jason's foul shots record increased by 8 is 30. Find his record.

2. Tina's weight decreased by 7 lb is 113 lb. Find her weight.

3. Fourteen increased by twice a number is 40. Find the number.

4. Seven less than 6 times a number is 43. Find the number.

5. The sum of 14 and 4 times a number is 38. Find the number.

6. The sum of twice a number and 24 is 38. Find the number.

7. Four less than 3 times the temperature is 41. Find the temperature.

8. The $80 selling price of a radio is $10 more than 5 times the cost. Find the cost.

9. Eight less than twice Rashid's age is 32. How old is Rashid?

10. $30 more than 3 times Hank's salary is $480. Find his salary.

11. Which problem below can be solved by the equation x + 5 =35?

    A. Marge was paid $35 for this week's part-time work as a maid. She got a $5.00 tip. How much money does she now have?

    B. Bert hiked 35 miles at 5 miles per hour. How long did he bike?

    C. Ron added 5 more stamps to his collection. If he now has 35 stamps in his collection, how many stamps did he have before he added the 5 more?

    D. By noon, a motel had 35 guests registered. Five more guests registered by 6:00 P.M. How many guests were then registered?

12. The equation 7x - 3 = 18 represents correctly the idea expressed in one of these sentences. Which sentence is it?

    A. 7 less than 3 times a number is 18.

    B. 3 less than 7 times a number is 18.

    C. 7 times 3 less than a number is 18.

    D. 3 more than 7 times a number is 18.

13. Which of the following problems can be solved by using the equation x + 5 = 19?

    A. Jose added 5 new tapes to his collection. If he now has 19 tapes in his collection, how many tapes did he have in his collection before adding the 5 new tapes?

    B. Donna has 19 guppies in her fish tank. She added 5 more. How many does she have now?

    C. Karen worked for two shifts at a restaurant on Friday. She earned $5 in tips during lunch and $19 in tips in supper hours. How much did she earn in tips that day?

    D. Sheena has five times as many pairs of earrings as Sonia. Sonia has 19 pairs of earrings. How many pairs of earrings does Sheena have?

14. The mean degree temperature for five days was 68. The degree temperatures were 60 on Monday, 70 on Tuesday, 80 on Wednesday, and 75 on Thursday. What was the temperature on Friday?

    A. 11   B. 55   C. 57   D. 70.6

15. Maureen's successful weekly foul shot totals in basketball were 15, 25, 30, 20, and 15. How many foul shots must she score in the sixth week to have an average of 20 for the six-week period?

    A. 15   B. 17.5   C. 20.8   D. 37.5

16.   Bill has an average of 80 on his first three English quizzes. What grade must he get on the fourth quiz to boost his average to 83?

    A. 80.75   B. 92   C. 96   D. 100

17.   Use the following information to choose the equation that will not solve the problem. Jack's average on four math tests is 89. What must he get on the fifth test to have an average of 90 on the five tests?

    (A) $4(89) + x = 450$

    (B) $356 + x = 90$

    (C) $\dfrac{4(89)}{5} + \dfrac{x}{5} = 90$

    (D) $\dfrac{4(89) + x}{5} = 90$

OPEN-ENDED QUESTION

18.   Two students asked to have their tests rescored. One student had a score of 50, which was far below the class average. The other had a score of 70, which was close to the class average. Willard believes that adding 20 points to the lower score would raise the class average more than adding 20 points to the higher score. Is Willard correct? Write a justification of your answer for someone who might disagree with you.

REVIEW

1.   Which of these groups of numbers correctly completes this table?

n	5(n - 4) + n
3	
	16

    A. -2 and 6   B. -18 and 6

    C. 8 and $\frac{2}{3}$ D. -38 and 16

2.   Evaluate $-4x + 3$ for $x = 2$.

    A. -11   B. -5   C. -3   D. 11

3.   Which of these is the closest approximation of $\sqrt{4020}$?

    A. 20.6   B. 63.4   C. 70.1   D. 2010

4. An assembly-line worker is packaging books in cartons for shipment of an order of 82 books to a school. If 7 books are placed in each carton, how many books would be left for the last carton?

    A. 6   B. 5   C. 4   D. 3

5. Todd, a star baseball player, gets a hit about $\frac{1}{3}$ of the time. If he batted 519 times, what should be his approximate total hitless at-bats?

    A. 106   B. 173   C. 346   D. 446

6. A $250 suit is advertised at $\frac{1}{5}$ off at Tops Clothes. The same suit is advertised at 25% off of its regular $260 price at Better Buys. How much is saved by buying at the lower price?

    A. $5   B. $10   C. $15   D. $195

7. Which of the following is a way to find 125% of a number?

    I   Multiply the number by 0.125.

    II   Add the number to $\frac{1}{4}$ of the number.

    III   Multiply the number by 1.25.

    IV   Multiply the number by 5 and then divide the result by 4.

    A.   I or II only   B. II, III, or IV only

    C.   II or IV only   D. I or IV only

8. What value of x makes x > 5 true?

    I $3 \cdot 2 - 1$

    II $\sqrt{36}$

    III   -50

    IV 2^3

    A. II or IV only   B. I or III only

    C. I or II only   D. I, II, or IV only

9. Which point on this number line represents the product of 3 and $-\frac{1}{2}$?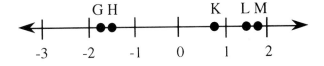

-105-

LESSON 13   PRE-ALGEBRA
Applications to Percent

You have learned to solve problems that involve finding a percent of a number. There are two other types of percent problems.

1. A number is **what** percent of a number?

   (A number is x% of a given number.)

2. A number is a given percent of **what** number?

   (A number is a given percent of **x**.)

You can use equations to solve any of these cases of percent.

EXAMPLE 1   4 is what percent of 6?

Strategy   Write the sentence as an equation.

4 is what % of 6?

$$4 = x \cdot 6$$ **Let x = the percent written as a decimal.**

$$4 = 6x$$

$$\frac{4}{6} = \frac{6x}{6}$$ **Divide each side by 6.**

$$\frac{2}{3} = x$$

Write $\frac{2}{3}$ as a decimal.

$$x = 0.66\frac{2}{3}$$

$$\begin{array}{r} 0.66 \quad \text{or } 0.66\frac{2}{3} \\ 3\overline{)2.00} \\ \underline{1\ 8} \\ 20 \\ \underline{18} \\ 2 \end{array}$$

$0.66\frac{2}{3}$ means $66\frac{2}{3}\%$

Solution   Thus, 4 is $\mathbf{66\frac{2}{3}}$ % of 6.

EXAMPLE 2   18 is 35% of what number?

Round your answer to the nearest whole number.

Strategy   Use the first sentence to write an equation.

(continued on next page)

-106-

Let **n** = the number.

18 is 35% of what **number** ?

18 = 0.35 ·   **n**

Solve   18 = 0.35n

$$\frac{18}{0.35} = \frac{0.35n}{0.35}$$

51.428571 = n   **18 ÷ 0.35 = 51.428571**

Now round 51.428571 to the nearest whole number.

   51.428571

   51   **4 is less than 5. So leave the 1 unchanged**

                 in rounding.

Solution   Thus, **51** is the number, rounded to the nearest whole number.

EXAMPLE 3   In basketball, good players make approximately 70% of their foul shots. Suppose that a good player missed 26 foul shot attempts during a season. Approximately how many foul shots did he attempt that season?

Strategy   The player missed 26 shots.

70% of the shots **made** means he made 70 out 100 shots.

Therefore, he **missed** 30 out of 100 shots, or **30%**.

To write an equation, express the given data in terms of **one** sentence.

Misses are 30% of attempts **OR** 30% of attempts are **misses**.

Either sentence will do. Use the first sentence to write an equation.

Misses are 30% of **A**ttempts.

26   = 0.30 · **A**   **Let A = number of attempts.**

Solve the equation.

    26   =   0.30A

86.666667   =   A   **Divide each side by 0.30.**

                  By calculator, 26 ÷ 0.30 = 86.666667.

Solution   He attempted approximately   **Round to the nearest whole number.**

87 foul shots.

EXAMPLE 4   Of the 200 bicycles at a vacation resort, 40 are not yet rented.
What percent of the 200 bicycles are rented?

Strategy   First find the number of bicycles already rented.

200 - number not yet rented   =   number already rented.

200 -   40   =   160

160 bicycles are rented.

Let x = the percent written as a decimal.

Now find **what** percent of 200 are rented. Write an equation.

$$x \cdot 200 = 160$$

$$200x = 160$$

$$x = 0.80 \quad \textbf{Divide each side by 200.}$$

By calculator, 160 ÷ 200 = 0.80.

Write 0.80 as a percent.

Solution   Thus, 80% of the bicycles are rented.

SUMMARY

How do you write an equation for each of the following?

1.   3 is what % of 7?   2. 6% of what number is 12?

3.   If 70% of the eighth grade class are boys, what percent are girls?

4.   If a basketball team won 75% of its games this season and there were no ties, what % of the games did the team lose?

5.   How do you solve the equation $2 = 5x$?
How do you write the solution as a percent?

6.   The eighth-grade class of 200 students has 120 boys.
Suppose you are asked: The number of girls is what percent of the class?
What must you do first to solve this problem?

SAMPLE EWT QUESTIONS

1. What % of 20 is 16?
   A. 8%   B. 32%   C. 80%   D. 125%

2. 240 is 30% of what number?
   A. 72   B. 80   C. 125   D. 800

3. 3% of what number is 12?
   A. 400   B. 40   C. 25   D. 0.36

4. 8 is what % of 2?
   A. 4%   B. 16%   C. 25%   D. 400%

5. Of the 300 golf clubs Monique has at her miniature golf stand, 60 are being used.
   What percent of the golf clubs are not being used?
   A. 20%   B. 25%   C. 18%   D. 80%

6. This year's football team played 15 games. The team lost 3 games. There were no ties.
   What percent of the games played did the team win?
   A. 8%   B. 20%   C. 45%   D. 80%

7. A baseball team loses 20% of its games. This season the team won 12 games.
   How many games did the team play if there were no ties?
   A. 15   B. 24   C. 60   D. 96

8. Jake usually makes a hit 30% of the times at bat. This season he failed to hit 14 times.
   How many times did he bat?
   A. 5   B. 20   C. 42   D. 47

9. Last week Jane ran 20 miles at track practice. This week she ran 25 miles.
   The increase is what percent of the number of miles she ran last week?
   A. 20%   B. 25%   C. 80%   D. 125%

10. The girls' basketball team score in last week's game was 30. They scored 24 in the game this week. The decrease was what percent of last week's score?

   A. 80%   B. 72%   C. 25%   D. 20%

11. A field hockey team won 80% of its games this season and there were no ties. The team lost 5 games. How many games did the team play?

12. Last week Jane earned $40.00 working part time. This week she earned $48.00 The increase this week is what % of last week's earnings?

13. Jan has a collection of 50 tapes and CDs. Of this collection, 5 are CDs What percent of the collection are tapes?

14. Of the 80 bicycles at the Rentabike shop, 20 are now being rented. What percent of the bikes are still available for rent?

The figure at the right shows a large rectangle divided into 7 small rectangles all the same size. Use this figure to answer Exercises 20-22 below.

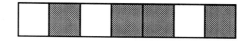

15. The number of unshaded rectangles is what % of the number of shaded rectangles?

16. The number of shaded rectangles is what % of the total number of rectangles?

17. The number of unshaded rectangles is what % of the total number of rectangles?

OPEN-ENDED QUESTION

18. For a sale, a store owner lowered the original price of a T.V. by 30%. After the sale, the store owner raised the price of that item by 30% of its sale price. A clerk in the store reasoned that the price would now be the same as before the first sale and marked the item at the original price. Did the clerk make a mistake? Justify your answer with an example of your own.

REVIEW

1. The sale price of a radio is the cost increased by 30%. If S represents the sale price and C represents the cost, Which formula describes how to find the sale price?
   A. $S = C - 30C$ B. $S = C + 0.30C$
   C. $S = 30C + C$ D. $S = C - 0.30C$

2. Juan's scores on four math tests were 70, 80, 70, and 70. What must he get on the fifth test to have an average of 74 for the five tests?
   A. 72.5   B. 72.8   C. 80   D. 91

3. The equation $3x + 5 = 10$ represents correctly the idea expressed in which one of the following sentences?
   A. 5 less than 3 times a number is 10.
   B. 10 more than 3 times number is 5.
   C. 5 more than 3 times a number is 10.
   D. 3 more than 5 times a number is 10.

4. Insert the appropriate inequality symbol to make -4.765 ? -4.785 true.
   A. >   B. <   C. =   D. You can't tell.

5. Evaluate $4x^3$ for $x = 2$.
   A. 10   B. 24   C. 32   D. 512

6. What digit is in the 23rd decimal place when $\frac{4}{7}$ is written as a decimal?

LESSON 14 PATTERNS AND RELATIONSHIPS
Numerical Patterns

Look at the sequence of numbers:

   4, 6, 8, 10, 12, ...

It is easy to see that the numbers are **increasing** by 2. That is, each number is 2 bigger than the number before it. So, the next number in the sequence will be 12 + **2**, or 14.

We call a sequence like this a ***number pattern***. Frequently, when the numbers are small, you can guess what the pattern is.

Other times it is helpful to look for a pattern involving a repeated arithmetic operation: addition, subtraction, multiplication, or division.

EXAMPLE 1   If the following pattern is continued, what will be the next number?
   3, 10, 17, 24, 31, ...

Strategy   First look for the simplest type of pattern. Look for a pattern that involves only **one** operation, like addition.

Test to see if the pattern is formed by addition.

Find the **difference** between each term and the next one.

   10 - 3 = **7**   17 - 10 = **7**   24 - 17 = **7**

The difference is always **7**.

This shows that you **add 7** to any number to get the next number.

   3 + **7** = 10   10 + **7** = 17   17 + **7** = 24   24 + **7** = 31

Solution   Therefore, the number following 31 in the sequence is 31 + **7** = 38.

EXAMPLE 2   Find the eighth term of this same sequence 3, 10, 17, 24, 31, ...

Strategy   In Example 1, above, you saw that **7** must be added to any number to get the next number in that sequence:

3,	10,	17,	24,	31,	31 + **7**,	38 + **7**,	45 + 7
1st	**2nd**	**3rd**	**4th**	**5th**	**6th**	**7th**	**8th**

Solution   Thus, the **8th** term of the sequence is 45 + 7, or **52**.

Sometimes **multiples** of a number play an important role in finding a number pattern.

What is meant by a **multiple** of some number, say, **7**?

Multiply 7 by any number, for example, **3**.

Recall that **multiplication** can be indicated by a **raised dot**.

$$7 \cdot 3 = 21 \qquad\qquad \textbf{7} \cdot \textbf{3 means 7 times 3.}$$

21 is called a **multiple** of 7.

EXAMPLE 3 What is the next number in the pattern 2, 6, 18, 54, ...?

Strategy First try subtraction of successive terms as you did in Example 1.

$$6 - 2 = \textbf{4} \qquad 18 - 6 = \textbf{12} \qquad 54 - 18 = \textbf{36}$$

You can see that the difference between successive terms is **NOT**

the same. So, the pattern is **NOT** formed by adding the same number.

If the pattern is not formed by addition, maybe it is formed by **multiplying**.

Test by **division** of successive terms:

$$6 \div 2 = \textbf{3} \qquad 18 \div 6 = \textbf{3} \qquad 54 \div 18 = \textbf{3}$$

Division works! The division shows that you **multiply** each number by **3** to get

the next number.

Solution Therefore, the number following 54 is $54 \cdot \textbf{3} = \textbf{162}$.

Some patterns involve **consecutive multiples** of a number.

Consecutive multiples of 3 are: 3, $\quad 3 \cdot 2, \quad 3 \cdot 3, \quad 3 \cdot 4, \quad 3 \cdot 5$, etc.

$$3, \qquad 6, \qquad 9, \qquad 12, \qquad 15$$

Also, sometimes numerical patterns involve geometric figures.

EXAMPLE 4 All faces of this die (one of a pair of dice) are numbered with consecutive multiples of 5. If no number is repeated, what numbers appear on the three hidden faces?

Strategy Write the three multiples shown in numerical order.

Are there any consecutive multiples **missing**?

(continued on next page)

The three multiples shown are 10, 15, and 35.

Note that consecutive multiples of 5 differ by 5.

For example, the next multiple of 5 after 10 is 10 + **5**, or 15.

Then adding 5 repeatedly, you get:

15 + **5** = 20

20 + **5** = 25

25 + **5** = 30

Solution   So, the numbers on the hidden faces are 20, 25, and 30.

Sometimes arithmetic pattern are connected to geometric figures, as shown in the next example.

EXAMPLE 5   If the pattern indicated in the three figures below were continued, how many pennies would be needed to form the seventh group of pennies?

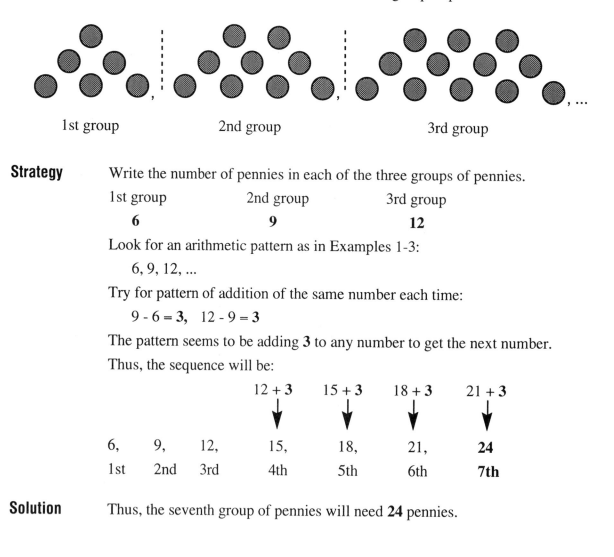

| 1st group | 2nd group | 3rd group |

Strategy   Write the number of pennies in each of the three groups of pennies.

1st group	2nd group	3rd group
6	**9**	**12**

Look for an arithmetic pattern as in Examples 1-3:

6, 9, 12, ...

Try for pattern of addition of the same number each time:

9 - 6 = **3**, 12 - 9 = **3**

The pattern seems to be adding **3** to any number to get the next number.

Thus, the sequence will be:

			12 + 3	15 + 3	18 + 3	21 + 3
			↓	↓	↓	↓
6,	9,	12,	15,	18,	21,	**24**
1st	2nd	3rd	4th	5th	6th	**7th**

Solution   Thus, the seventh group of pennies will need **24** pennies.

DISCOVERY   A thirteenth-century mathematician named Leonardo Fibonacci came up with the following sequence of numbers: 1, 1, 2, 3, 5, 8, 13, **...** . This is called the **Fibonacci Sequence**.

What is the next term in this sequence?

The next example involves this type of pattern.

EXAMPLE 6   What is the next number in the sequence 5, 7, 12 19, 31, ... ?

Strategy   Note that 12, the third number in the sequence, is the sum of the previous two numbers, 5 and 7. And so forth.

5, 7, 12, 19, 31,	$12 = 5 + 7$
5, 7, **12,** 19, 31	$19 = 7 + 12$
5, 7, **12, 19,** 31	$31 = 12 + 19$

Solution   Therefore, the next number in the sequence must be $19 + 31 = \mathbf{50}$.

EXAMPLE 7   A school library is equipped with several small square tables. Each table can accommodate exactly one person per side. If two tables are joined, the resulting table can accommodate exactly 6 people. If three of these tables are placed end-to-end, the resulting table can accommodate exactly 8 people.

If eight of these tables are lined up end-to-end, how many people can the resulting table can accommodate?

Strategy   Study the pattern for **5** tables:

Total number of people at **5** tables is:

$$2 \cdot 5 \quad + \quad 2$$
$$10 \quad + \quad 2$$
$$12$$

The number of people at 5 tables is 12.

5 people

1 person at each end

1 person at each end

5 people

Solution   Similarly, the number of people at **8** tables is $2 \cdot 8 + 2 = 16 + 2 = \mathbf{18}$

-115-

The next pattern involves the idea of **ratio.**

You will study ratio in greater detail in the next lesson.

Ratio is used to compare two numbers.

This figure shows 3 unshaded squares and 5 shaded squares.

The ratio of **unshaded** to **shaded** squares is

     3   to   **5**, written as

        3 : 5 or as a fraction

        $\frac{3}{5}$

EXAMPLE 8   If this pattern were continued, what would be the ratio of the number of small unshaded triangles to the number of small shaded triangles in the next figure in the pattern?

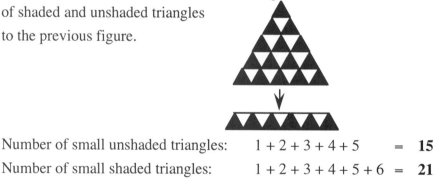

1st group   2nd group   3rd group

Strategy   Notice, each group of triangles is formed by adding **one** more row of shaded and unshaded triangles to the previous figure.

Next figure: 3rd group with one more row of triangles added.

Number of small unshaded triangles: $1 + 2 + 3 + 4 + 5$ = **15**

Number of small shaded triangles: $1 + 2 + 3 + 4 + 5 + 6$ = **21**

Solution   Thus the ratio of the number of small shaded triangles in the next figure in the pattern is $\frac{15}{21}$, or $\frac{5}{7}$.

SUMMARY

What is the strategy for finding the next term in each sequence?

1. 7, 10, 13, 16, ...

2. 2, 8, 32, 128, ...

3. 2, 2, 4, 6, 10, 16, ...

4. How do you find the 3 missing multiples in the following set of 6 multiples of 4: 8, 12, 28?

Use the figure below to answer Exercises 5-8.

5. How can you determine the pattern of the figure?

6. Describe the pattern.

7. How can you predict the total number of blocks in the fourth figure if the pattern continues?

8. How can you use the pattern to predict the total number of blocks in the sixth figure if the pattern continues?

9. A rectangular table can seat one person at each end and two people at each side. Explain the strategy for determining the number of people who can be seated if three of these tables are placed end-to-end.

10. What is the ratio of the number of small shaded squares to the number of small unshaded squares?

SAMPLE EWT QUESTIONS

Find the next term in each sequence.

1. 2, 4, 6, 8, 10, ...

2. 5, 8, 11, 14, 17, ...

3. 15, 12, 9, 6, ...

4. 24, 20, 16, 12, 8, ...

5. 1, 2, 4, 8, 16, ...

6. 1, 5, 25, 125, ...

7. 3, 3, 6, 9, 15, 24, ...

8. 7, 9, 16, 25, 41, 66, ...

Use a calculator to find the next term in each sequence.

9. 378, 677, 976, 1275, ...

10. 49, 1127, 25921, 596183, ...

11. All faces of this box or die are numbered with consecutive multiples of 7. If no number is repeated, what numbers appear on the three hidden faces?

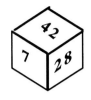

A. 28, 35, 49   B. 14, 21, 35   C. 14, 28, 56   D. 7, 14, 21

12. All faces of this box or die are numbered with consecutive multiples of 8. If no number is repeated, what numbers appear on the three hidden faces?

A. 24, 32, 48   B. 8, 16, 24   C. 48, 56, 64   D. 24, 32, 40

If the patterns shown below are continued, how many squares will be in the sixth figure? (Exercises 13 - 14)

13.

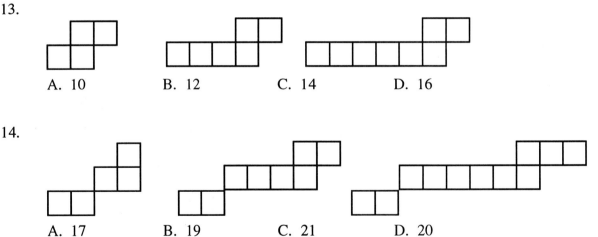

A. 10   B. 12   C. 14   D. 16

14.

A. 17   B. 19   C. 21   D. 20

15. If the pattern below were continued, how many blocks would be in the sixth figure?

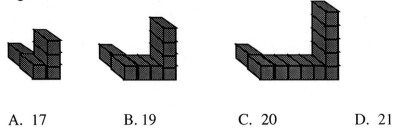

A. 17   B. 19   C. 20   D. 21

16. A cafeteria is equipped with square tables that seat exactly one person at each side.
    If 15 of these tables are placed end-to-end, how many people can the resulting table seat?
    A. 16   B. 30   C. 31   D. 32

17. A hotel meeting room is equipped with rectangular tables that can seat 1 person at
    each end and 4 people at each of the sides. How many people can be seated if 6 of these
    tables are placed end-to-end?

18. This figure consists of
    alternating light and dark
    squares. By how much does
    the number of dark squares
    exceed the number of light
    squares?

SAME PATTERN HERE

19. If this pattern were continued, what
    would be the ratio of the number of
    small unshaded squares to the
    number of small shaded squares in the
    next group in the pattern?

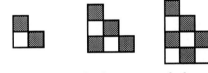

1st group   2nd group   3rd group

20. If this pattern were continued, what
    would be the ratio of the number of
    small unshaded triangles to the total
    number of small triangles in the fifth
    group in the pattern?

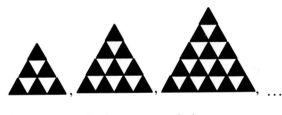

1st group   2nd group   3rd group

OPEN-ENDED QUESTION

21. Use each of the digits 3, 4, 5, 6, 7, and 8 <u>once and only once</u> to form two three-digit
    numbers that will give the largest possible sum when they are added. Show your work. Is
    more than one answer possible? Explain your answer.

REVIEW

1.   A field hockey team loses 20% of it games. This season, the team won 12 games. How many games did the team lose if there were no ties?
     A. 3   B. 15   C. 24   D. 60

2.   Last week Jane earned $40 at a part-time job. This week she earned $50. The increase is what percent of last week's earnngs?
     A. 20%   B. 25%   C. 80%   D. 125%

Use this table to answer Exercises 3-6 below.

Enrollment of 200 of 300 Eighth Graders in Introductory Foreign Language Courses		
Course	Girls	Boys
Spanish	50	20
French	20	30
Latin	40	10
German	20	?

3.   How many boys are enrolled in German?
     A. 40   B. 30   C. 20   D. 10

4.   The number of girls in Spanish is how much more than the number of boys in Spanish?
     A. 10   B. 30   C. 50   D. 70

5.   The number of girls in Latin is what percent of the number of girls in Spanish?
     A. 10%   B. 20%   C. 80%   D. 125%

6.   What is the average of the number of girls in all foreign language classes?
     A. 130   B. 65   C. 32.5   D. 17.5

7.   Travis packs exactly 7 books in a carton for shipping. Since he began, he has packed a total of 87 books. How many full cartons has he packed so far?
     A. 3   B. 12   C. 13   D. 84

8.   Every fifteen minutes, the number of bacteria in a science experiment approximately doubles. The population at 3 P.M. was about one quarter of a million bacteria. Find the approximate size of the population at 6 P.M.

LESSON 15 PATTERNS AND RELATIONSHIPS
Repeating Blocks of Symbols

In Lesson 14, you worked with patterns of numbers. This lesson is about another kind of pattern you will find on the EWT. In this kind of pattern, a block of symbols repeats over and over.

Example 1 illustrates this sort of pattern. With symbol patterns like this, the question often asks which of the symbols will be in a particular position.

EXAMPLE 1   Examine this pattern:

EWTMATHEWTMATHEWTMATH...

If this pattern keeps repeating, which symbol will be in the 17th position?

Strategy   This pattern consists of a block of letters repeated over and over: **EWTMATH**. Each block contains **7** symbols. So it repeats in groups of 7.

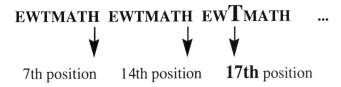

EWTMATH EWTMATH EW**T**MATH   ...

7th position   14th position   **17th** position

But suppose you want to find what symbol is in the 17th position without counting. You could divide **17** by **7**—the number of symbols in one block. The answer is 2 with a **remainder of 3**.

The remainder is what counts here.
It tells you that the symbol you want is the **3rd** symbol after the second block—the letter **T**.
Look at the diagram above to see why this is so.

Solution   Either way, the symbol in the 17th position is **T**.

EXAMPLE 2   What symbol is in the 165th position of **EWTMATHEWTMATH...** ?

Strategy   Divide 165 by 7, the number of symbols in each repeating block.

The division shows that the block of symbols
is repeated 23 times with remainder of **4**.
The fourth symbol in the block **EWTMATH** is **M**.

$$\begin{array}{r} 23 \\ 7\overline{)165} \\ \underline{14} \\ 25 \\ \underline{21} \\ \mathbf{4} \end{array}$$

Solution   Therefore, **M** is in the 165th position.

Some patterns involve exponents. We first review the idea of **digits** of a number.

For example, for the number 136:   **1** is the **hundreds** digit.

3 is the **tens** digit.

6 is the **units** digit.

EXAMPLE 3   What is the units digit in the 95th term of the sequence $3^1, 3^2, 3^3, 3^4, ...$?

Strategy   First look for a pattern of the units digits of successive terms.

Write out several terms in the sequence.

$$3^1 = 3, \qquad 3^2 = 9, \qquad 3^3 = 27, \text{ etc.}$$

The values of the terms from 3^1 to 3^8 are

3, 9, 27, 81, 243, 729, 2187, and 6561.

There is a pattern in the **units** digits (**blackened in below**).

3, 9, 27, 81,   **24**3, **72**9, **218**7, **656**1

They repeat in blocks of 4 digits: **3, 9, 7, 1**:

Number $3^1, \quad 3^2, \quad 3^3, \quad 3^4, \quad 3^5, \quad 3^6, \quad 3^7, \quad 3^8, ...$

	1st	2nd	3rd	4th	5th	6th	7th	8th
Units digit of number	3	9	7	1	3	9	7	1 ,....

There are 4 digits in a block. So divide 95 by **4**.
The division shows that the block of units
digits repeats 23 times with **3** left over.
The 3rd digit in the block **3971** is **7**.

$$\begin{array}{r} 23 \\ 4\overline{)95} \\ \underline{8} \\ 15 \\ \underline{12} \\ \mathbf{3} \text{ remainder} \end{array}$$

Solution   Therefore, **7** is the units digit of the 95th term.

Sometimes, repeating blocks of symbols are geometric. One such pattern occurs in the **spiral** of the next example.

EXAMPLE 4   The spiral below indicates a repeating pattern.

Which symbols are missing from the pattern at the positions x and y?

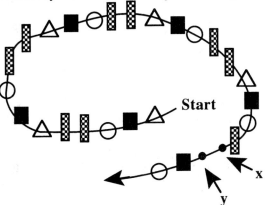

Strategy   First find the repeating pattern. What marks its beginning and end?

What block of symbols is being repeated over and over?

The pattern is displayed below.

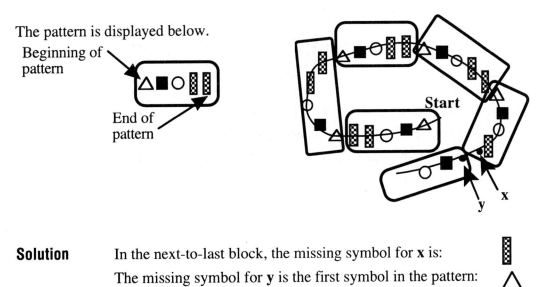

Solution   In the next-to-last block, the missing symbol for **x** is:

The missing symbol for **y** is the first symbol in the pattern:

Sometimes a pattern like the spiral of Example 4 is altered by a slight, but consistent, change each time the pattern is repeated. For example, every time a block of figures is repeated, an extra triangle or circle is added. Then the problem becomes a combination of **geometric** and **arithmetic** patterns. This is illustrated in the next example.

EXAMPLE 5   Which symbols are missing from the pattern at the positions x and y?

■ △ ▦ ○ ■ △ ▦ ○○ ■ △ ▦ ○○○ ■△▦ ○○○ ? ?

↑ ↑
x y

Strategy   First look for a repetitive pattern.

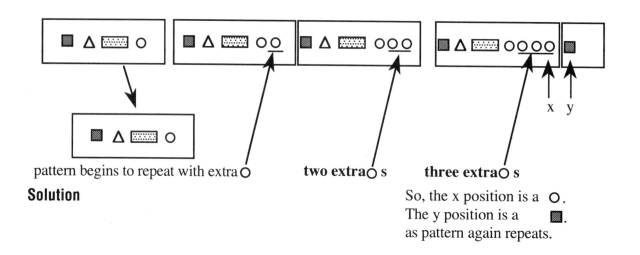

pattern begins to repeat with extra ○

two extra ○s   **three extra ○s**

Solution

So, the x position is a ○.
The y position is a ■.
as pattern again repeats.

The next pattern is an unusual number pattern that frequently occurs on standardized tests. It might very well appear in the next EWT.

Consider the following numbers.:

The number 424 reads the same backward as forward.

The number 13731 reads the same backward as forward.

The number 59995 reads the same backward as forward.

Numbers like these are called **palindrome** numbers. An EWT question may give you a palindrome number and ask you what the next palindrome number is.

The next examples illustrate a strategy for working with a **palindrome** with a **single middle digit NOT 9** (for example, 43735) or with several middle digits **NOT 9**: (for example, 4**88**4).

EXAMPLE 6   Find the next palindrome number after 32723.

Strategy   For the palindrome 32723   **7** is the middle digit.

↓

Next palindrome: 32**8**23   Add 1 to **7** to get the next palindrome.

Solution   So, the next palindrome after 32723 is **32823**.

EXAMPLE 7   Find the next palindrome number after 6336.

Strategy   For the palindrome   6 [33] 6   there are two **middle digits: 33.**

Next palindrome: 6 [44] 6   Add **11** to 33 to get the next palindrome.

Solution   So, the next palindrome after 6336 is **6446**.

Trial and error will lead you to discover the pattern for palindromes with middle digit 9 or several middle digits 9. Consider the palindrome 494. Bigger numbers 495, 496, 497, 498, and 499 are **NOT** palindromes.

So, the next palindrome must be a number in the 500s.

The first number in the 500s that is a palindrome is **505**.

Notice the pattern.   palindrome   494

next palindrome   **505**   **The middle digit 9 is changed to a 0.**
1 is added to the digit on either side.

EXAMPLE 8   Find the next palindrome after 2799972.

Strategy   palindrome: 2799972
2800082   **Change 9s to 0s.**
Add 1 to each 7.

Solution   Thus, the next palindrome after 2799971 is **2800082**.

SUMMARY

1.   Explain the strategy for determining which symbol will be in the 53rd position for the following pattern: **largerlargerlarger...**

2.   How can you find the units digit in the 63rd term of the sequence $3^1, 3^2, 3^3, 3^4, ...$?

3.   What is a palindrome number?

4.   How do you find the next palindrome number after the palindrome 1499941?

5. How can you determine the pattern for this spiral?

6. How can you then use this pattern to find the missing symbols for positions x and y?

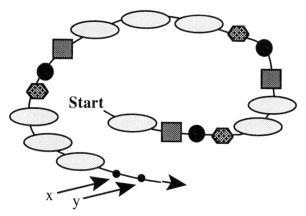

SAMPLE EWT QUESTIONS

For each of the following, if the pattern is continued, what symbol will be in the indicated position? (Exercises 1-4)

1. **trianglestrianglestriangles...**   51th position
   A. a   B. g   C. t   D. l

2. **exponentexponentexponent...**   107th position
   A. x   B. o   C. p   D. e

3. **HSPT11HSPT11HSPT11...**   47th position
   A. 1   B. H   C. T   D. P

4. **ALGEBRA1ALGEBRA1ALGEBRA1...**   58th position
   A. 1   B. A   C. B   D. L

5. What is the units digit in the 114th term of the sequence $7^1, 7^2, 7^3, 7^4, ...$?
   A. 9   B. 7   C. 3   D. 1

6. What is the units digit in the 131st term of the sequence $8^1, 8^2, 8^3, 8^4, ...$?
   A. 2   B. 4   C. 6   D. 8

7. What is the units digit in the 107th term of the sequence $3^1, 3^2, 3^3, 3^4, ...$?
   A. 9   B. 7   C. 3   D. 1

For each palindrome number, find the next larger palindrome number.

8.   343
9.   5665
10.   432666234
11.   3569653
12.   4699964
13.   934999439

Recall that one type of pattern involves repeating decimals.

Write the fraction $\frac{5}{7}$ as a decimal. Divide 7 into 5.000000 000000 00000

$$\frac{0.714285\ 714285\ 714285}{7)\overline{5.000000\ 000000\ 000000}}$$

The quotient (answer) **repeats** in blocks of 6 digits. The block **714285** repeats forever.

This is indicated in mathematics by writing a **bar** over the digits that repeat. $\frac{5}{7} = 0.\overline{714285}$.

14.   What is the digit in the 50th decimal place of the repeating decimal $0.\overline{325614}$?

15.   What is the digit in the 45th decimal place of the repeating decimal $0.\overline{4235698}$?

What symbols are missing from each pattern below at the locations x and y? (Exercises 16-17)

16.   17.

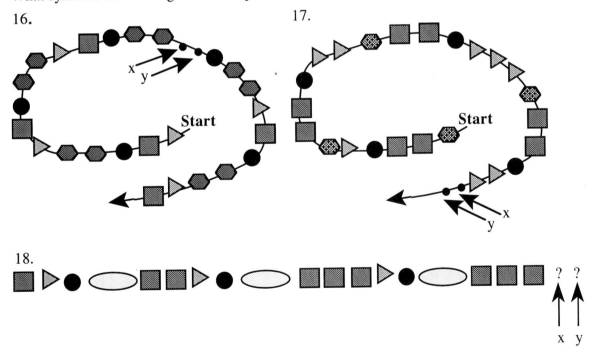

18.

-127-

OPEN-ENDED QUESTION

19. If the pattern along three diagonals below is continued, describe what will be contained in a fourth diagonal of figures. Explain how you came to your conclusion.

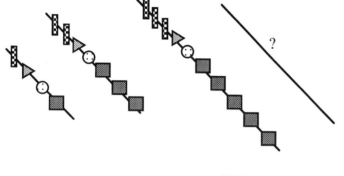

REVIEW

1. A T.V. that regularly sells for $400 is on sale at a 25% discount.
   Which of the procedures below could you use to find the sale price?

   I $400 \cdot 0.25$ II $400 \cdot 0.75$

   III $400 - 0.25 \cdot 400$ IV $400 - \frac{1}{4} \cdot 400$

   A. I only   B. I or II only   C. II, III, or IV only   D. III only

2. Which of the following is <u>not</u> equal to the others?

   A. $8 \div \frac{1}{2}$ B. $8 \cdot 3 - 8$ C. 2^4 D. $\sqrt{32}$

3. Which of these whole numbers most closely approximates $7\frac{4}{5} + 8\frac{1}{4} + 6\frac{7}{8}$?

   A. 21   B. 22   C. 23   D. 24

4. Insert two fractions between $\frac{1}{2}$ and $\frac{1}{8}$.

5. Which number has all the following characteristics?
   - It is a prime number
   - It is greater than 20
   - It is less than 30
   - It does not have a 9 in its units place.

LESSON 16 PATTERNS AND RELATIONSHIPS
Visualizing in Three Dimensions

Many patterns in mathematics involve three-dimensional visualization. You will now take a look at one such pattern.

The example below shows three views of a die. The digits 1-6 appear exactly once on the faces of this die. You will be asked to predict which number must be on a face you cannot see.

EXAMPLE 1   What number is
opposite the 5?

What number is
opposite the 1?

What number is
opposite the 2?

1st view   2nd view   3rd view

Strategy   Notice that the **2** is on the top in all three views.

Let's think of **1** as the **front** of the die and label the other faces in
terms of the front and top.

1st view   **2nd view**   **3rd view**

The **left** is opposite the right.   The **back** is opposite the front.

6 is opposite 5.   **3** is opposite 1.

The **bottom** is opposite the top.

Solution   **4** is the only number remaining. Therefore, **4** is opposite 2.

NOTE: It might help to visualize the work above by first tracing the figure
at the right. Cut it out. Fold up the faces to form a die. Tape the edges
together. This now shows you the 1st view above. Use the other two views
to write the correct numbers for the remaining 3 faces of the die.

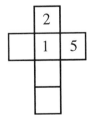

The box at the right can be formed by drawing a plane figure and folding up its sides. The shape of the plane figure can be discovered by cutting along certain edges of this box, folding up sides or faces to form a single plane figure. This is illustrated below.

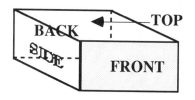

Cut along the bottom edge and the two vertical edges of the **FRONT** of the box. Fold up the **FRONT** flap of the box.

Repeat the process above for the **BACK** flap of the box.

Cut along the right edge of the **BOTTOM** of the box. Fold the **BOTTOM** down in line with the **LEFT SIDE** of the box.

Finally, fold up the **remaining** flaps in line with the **TOP** of the box.

These figures are **slanted** to give the drawings a 3-dimensional look. An unslanted version of the plane figure that would fold into a box is shown on the next page.

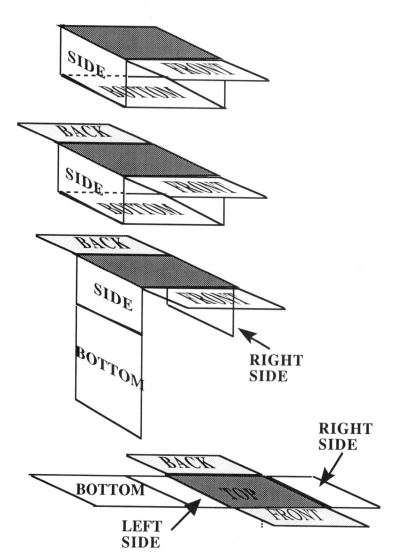

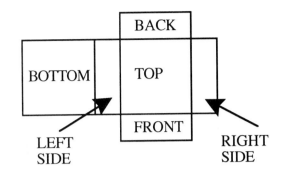

Notice the following pattern.

The front and back are **not** joined.

The sides are **not** joined.

The top and bottom are **not** joined.

It is sometimes difficult to visualize how the plane figure above could actually fold into a box. It may be helpful to actually do the folding so you can see that it really works.

MANIPULATIVE DISCOVERY

Trace each of the figures below on a sheet of tracing paper.

(Your teacher may give you an enlarged copy.)

Cut out each figure.

Fold along the dotted lines to try to form a box that can be taped together.

Which figure can be formed into a box?

Can you explain why the other figure does not work?

FIGURE (A)

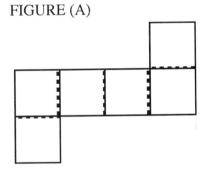

FIGURE (B)

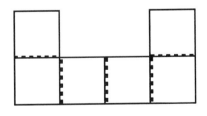

EXAMPLE 2   Which of the plane figures below cannot be folded to form a box?

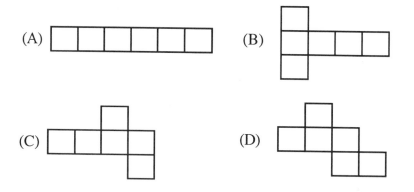

(A)   (B)

(C)   (D)

Strategy   The squares in Figure (A) are all strung out in a row. There are no squares that will close up the box. If you continue folding you will always find two sides of the box left over that cannot close up the box.

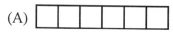

(A)

Box is missing front and back.

Below is an illustration of how Figure (D) can be folded to form a box.

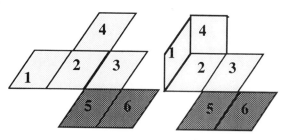

Fold 1 and 4 up.   Fold 3, 5, and 6 up.   Fold 5 and 6 to the left.   Fold 6 down.

Solution   Similarly, Figures (B) and (C) can be folded to produce a box. Therefore, Figure (A) is the only one that cannot be folded to produce a box.

EXAMPLE 3   The plane figure at the right can be folded into a box. Which of the figures below is a possible view of the box after it is constructed ?

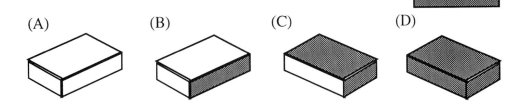

(A)   (B)   (C)   (D)

Strategy   Note that when the pattern is folded, the figure it forms will have three gray surfaces.

Two of the gray surfaces will be the top and the bottom. Of course, you won't be able to see the one on the bottom.

Only one **short** narrow side is shaded gray.

Also notice that **NEITHER** of the **long** narrow surfaces is shaded gray.

So Figure (A) is wrong. The top (large wide surface) is **not shaded gray.** Since both of the large wide surfaces in the original pattern are shaded gray, any large wide surface must be shaded gray in the 3-D drawing.

Figures (B) and (D) are not possible since each displays a long narrow side that is shaded gray.

This leaves Figure (C) as the remaining choice.

Figure (C) displays a **short narrow** side and a **large wide** surface that are **shaded gray**.

Assume that the other large wide surface that cannot be seen, the bottom of the box, is **shaded gray**. Also assume that the other short narrow side is not shaded gray.

Solution   Therefore, (C) is the only possible figure.

The explanation demonstrated in Example 3 above illustrates an important technique in answering multiple-choice questions. First try to eliminate impossible choices. If there are 4 multiple choices, elimination of three of them implies that the fourth choice must be correct.

SUMMARY

At the right are three views of a die. The digits 1-6 appear exactly once on the faces of this die.

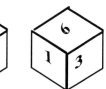

1st view   2nd view   3rd view

1. What digit is on the top face of the die?

2. What digit is in the front of the die?

3. How do you find the number opposite the 3?

4. Tell how to fold the plane figure at the right to make a box?

	6		
1	2	3	4
	5		

SAMPLE EWT QUESTIONS

At the right are three views of a die. The digits 1-6 appear exactly once on the faces of this die.

1. What digit is opposite 5?
2. What digit is opposite 3?
3. What digit is opposite 2?

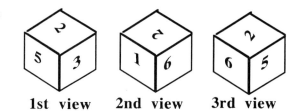

1st view   2nd view   3rd view

The letters A, B, C, D, E, and F appear exactly once on the faces of three views of a die.

4. What letter is opposite F?
5. What letter is opposite D?
6. What letter is opposite C?

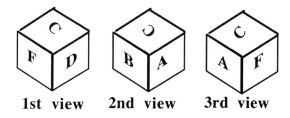

1st view   2nd view   3rd view

At the right are three views of a die.
The digits 1-6 appear exactly once on the
faces of this die.

7.   What digit is opposite 5?

8.   What digit is opposite 3?

9.   What digit is opposite 2?

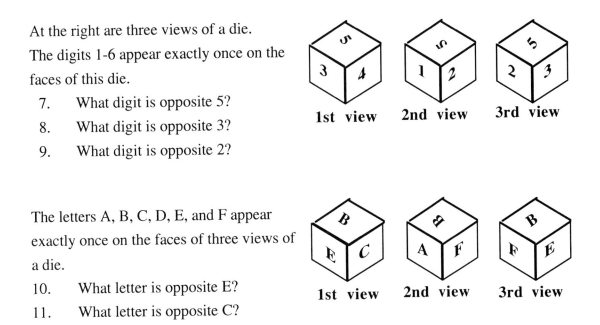

1st view   **2nd view**   **3rd view**

The letters A, B, C, D, E, and F appear
exactly once on the faces of three views of
a die.

10.   What letter is opposite E?

11.   What letter is opposite C?

12.   What letter is opposite B?

1st view   **2nd view**   **3rd view**

Which of the plane figures below cannot be folded to form a box or cube? (Ex. 13-16)

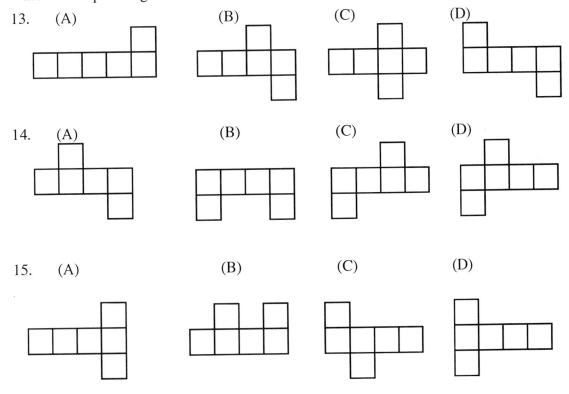

13.   (A)   (B)   (C)   (D)

14.   (A)   (B)   (C)   (D)

15.   (A)   (B)   (C)   (D)

16.   (A)   (B)   (C)   (D)

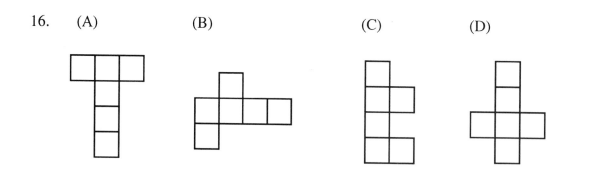

If the plane figure on the left is folded to form a box, which figure on the right is a possibile view of that box? (Ex. 17-21)

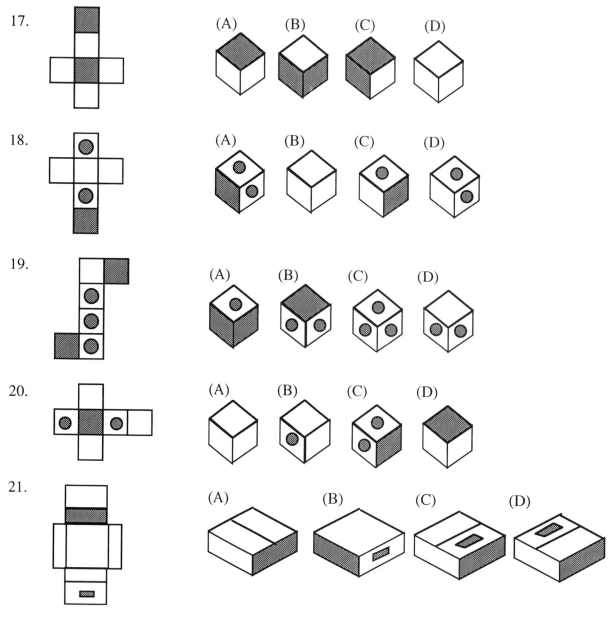

17.   (A)   (B)   (C)   (D)

18.   (A)   (B)   (C)   (D)

19.   (A)   (B)   (C)   (D)

20.   (A)   (B)   (C)   (D)

21.   (A)   (B)   (C)   (D)

To the right of each pattern in Exercises 22–23 there are four 3-dimensional figures.
Which figure is the result of folding the pattern shown?

22.

(A) (B) (C) (D)

23.

(A) (B) (C) (D)

24.   Suppose that the flat paper shape shown below were folded along the dotted lines to form
a box like the one pictured at the right. Which of the shapes below would be on the top of
the box if the black dot were on the bottom?

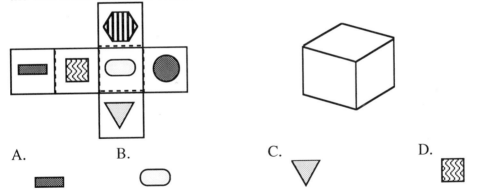

A.   B.   C.   D.

OPEN-ENDED QUESTION

25.   The cube at the right has a number on each of its six faces. If
the sum of the numbers on each pair of opposite faces is 10,
what is the sum of the numbers on the faces not shown?

Write an explanation of how you got your answer.

-137-

REVIEW

1. Barry mistakenly divided by 12 instead of multiplying by 12 while using his calculator. If the incorrect answer displayed on the calculator screen is 60, what is the correct answer?

    A. 5   B. 720   C. 8640   D. none of these

2. Which point on this number line best represents the product of 7 and $-\frac{1}{4}$?

    A. M   B. K

    C. G   D. H

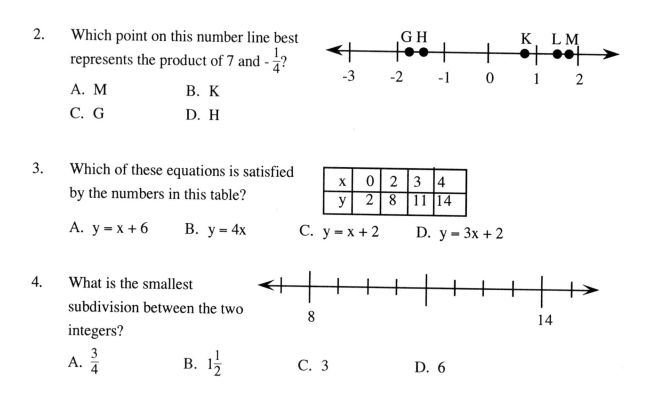

3. Which of these equations is satisfied by the numbers in this table?

x	0	2	3	4
y	2	8	11	14

    A. $y = x + 6$ B. $y = 4x$ C. $y = x + 2$ D. $y = 3x + 2$

4. What is the smallest subdivision between the two integers?

    A. $\frac{3}{4}$ B. $1\frac{1}{2}$ C. 3   D. 6

5. During a cold winter week the temperature fell 7°, rose 3°, fell 6°, and then rose 8°. If the temperature was 29° at the beginning of the week, what was it at the end of the five days?

6. Evaluate $3x + 2$ for $x = -4$.

7. Solve $7 + 2(5x + 2) = 31$.

LESSON 17 PATTERNS AND RELATIONSHIPS
Coordinates in a Plane

The figure at the right shows a part of
a sheet of **graph paper**.

The two number lines are called the
    x-axis (**horizontal number line**)
        and the
    y-axis (**vertical number line**).

The point where the **axes** meet is
called the **origin**.

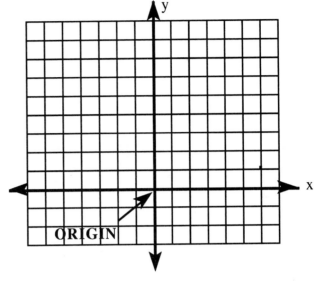

Points can be located in terms of
movement **left (negative)** or **right (positive)**.
movement **down (negative)** or **up (positive)**.

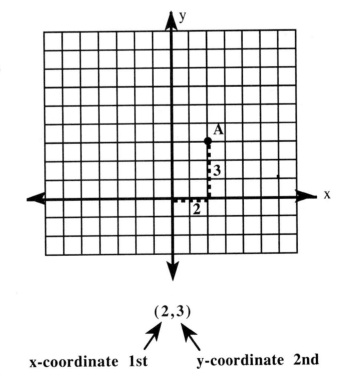

Here's how to get to Point A on this
graph:

• Start at the origin.

• Move **2** units to the **right** along
   the **x-axis**.

• Move **3** units **up**.

We say that Point A is at
coordinates (2,3).

The **order** of the coordinates of the
point is very important.

(2,3)

x-coordinate 1st   y-coordinate 2nd

-139-

EXAMPLE 1   Find the coordinates of the points shown on the graphs.

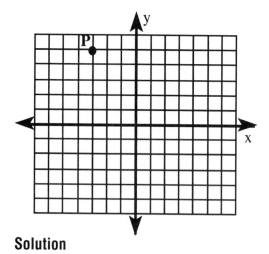
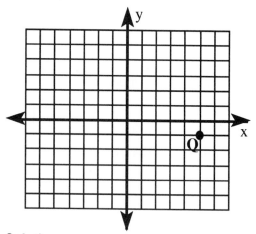

Solution

From the origin, move **left 3**, **up 5**.

(-3,5)

Solution

From the origin, move **right 5**, **down 1**.

(5,-1)

EXAMPLE 2   Give the coordinates of points T, A, and B.

For each point, begin at the origin.

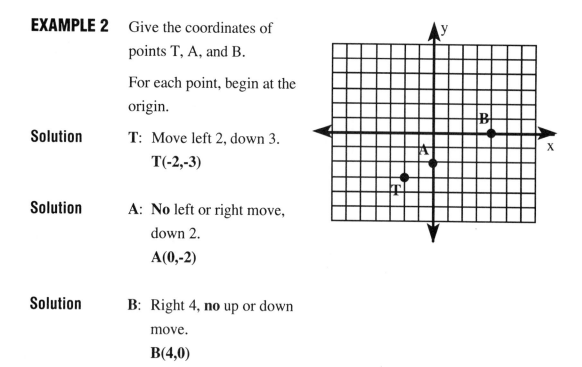

Solution   T: Move left 2, down 3.

T(-2,-3)

Solution   A: **No** left or right move, down 2.

A(0,-2)

Solution   B: Right 4, **no** up or down move.

B(4,0)

You have seen how to name the coordinates of a point already graphed.

In the next example you will be given the coordinates of a point. Then you will see how to graph this point.

EXAMPLE 3 Graph the points S(-2,0) and G(3,-2).

Strategy for S(-2,0)

For S, begin at the origin.

    Move **left 2** along the x-axis.

    Do not move up or down.

Put a dot at the point.

Label the point S(-2,0).

Strategy for G(3,-2)

For G, begin at the origin.

    Move **right 3** along the x-axis.

    Then move **down 2**.

Put a dot at the point.

Label the point G(3,-2).

Solution

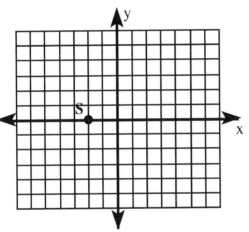

Solution

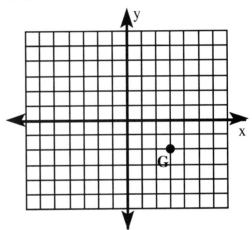

Points on a graph are said to represent a **linear relationship** if they all lie on a line.

The graph at the right shows how much Pat and Frank earned for hours worked.

Notice that the points for Frank are all on a **line**. This shows a *linear* relationship between hours worked and dollars earned for Frank.

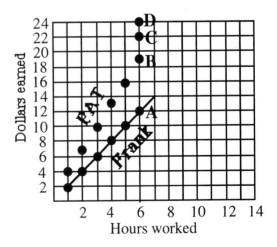

The points for Pat"s earnings represent a linear relationship, too.

    How can you show this?

    Which point—B, C, or D—is on the line

        for Pat's earnings??

This is explained in the next example.

EXAMPLE 4   Using the graph from the bottom of the previous page, determine the amount Pat earns for 6 hours work.

Strategy

Put a ruler along the points for Pat.

It might help to trace the graph on tracing paper and then actually draw the line through the points for Pat.

You will see that the line goes through Point B, not Points C and D.

In the second drawing, we omit the points for Frank to make it easier to see what Pat earns. We are interested only in the points for Pat.

1.   Start at 6 on the hours axis.
2.   Move straight up to point B, the only lettered point that is on the line for Pat's points.
3.   Read across horizontally to the left to the dollars axis.

It looks like the number is halfway between 18 and 20. That number is 19:

$$\frac{18+20}{2} = \frac{38}{2} = 19.$$

Solution   Thus, Pat earns $19 for 6 hours work.

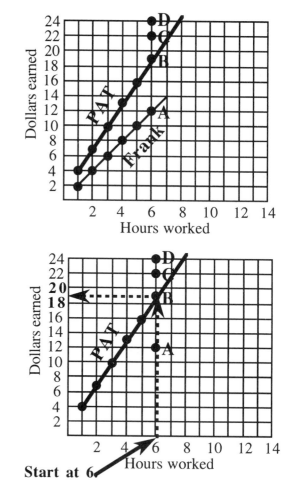

EXAMPLE 5   You are playing a game in which you are asked to pick a point according to a pattern. You always pick your next point by taking your last point and increasing the x-coordinate by 4 and decreasing the y-coordinate by 5. Find the coordinates of the point you will pick on your next turn after picking the point S.

(continued on next page)

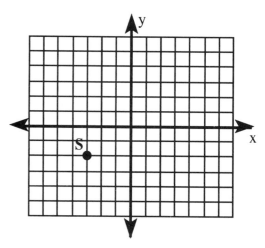

Strategy   First use the graph at the bottom of the previous page to find the coordinates of the point S.

Points: (-3,-2)   **From the origin move 3 left, 2 down.**

So, **x = -3** and **y = -2**.

New point: **x**   increased by 4   **y**   decreased by 5

     -3 [increased by] 4   **-2** [decreased by] 5

     -3   [+ 4]   -2   [+ (-5)]

          1   **-7**

Solution   Thus, the new point will be **(1,-7)**.

EXAMPLE 6   Which of the graphs below correctly represents the relationship indicated in the table?

Rectangles with Perimeters of 20 Units

Length	1	2	3	4	5	6	7	8	9
Width	9	8	7	6	5	4	3	2	1

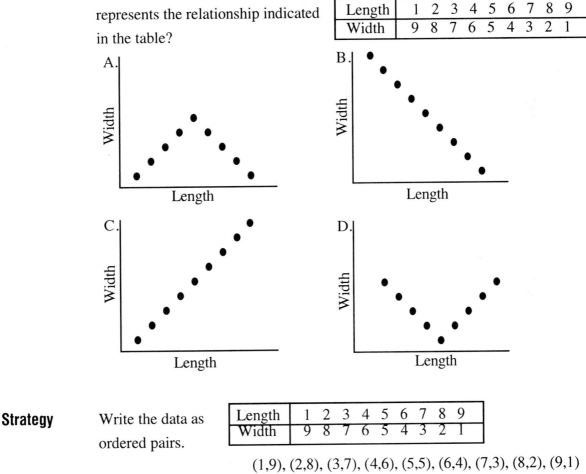

Strategy   Write the data as ordered pairs.

Length	1	2	3	4	5	6	7	8	9
Width	9	8	7	6	5	4	3	2	1

(1,9), (2,8), (3,7), (4,6), (5,5), (6,4), (7,3), (8,2), (9,1)

Plot these points on graph paper. Check which graph above seems to match the graph you have drawn.

(continued on next page)

-143-

The graph drawn at the right most closely approximates the graph of Choice B on the previous page.

Length	1	2	3	4	5	6	7	8	9
Width	9	8	7	6	5	4	3	2	1

Solution Thus, Choice B correctly represents the relationship indicated in the table.

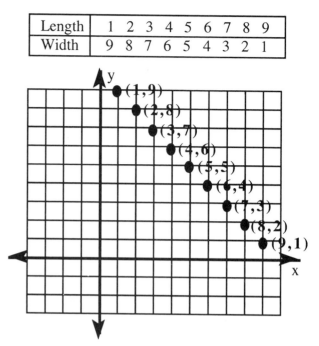

SUMMARY

Tell how to graph each of the following points.

1. A(-4,-2)   2. B(5,-3)   3. C(-8,1)   4. D(1,5)

5. E(-4,0)   6. F(0,-6)   7. G(0,10)   8. H(3,0)

Tell how to write the coordinates of the points graphed below.

9. P   10. Q

11. R   12. S

13. T   14. U

15. V   16. W

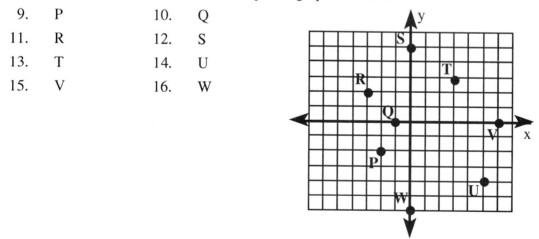

17. Plot the point T(-4,3). How do you find the coordinates of the point formed by increasing the x-coordinate of point T by 6 and decreasing the y-coordinate by 5.

The graph at the right shows the number of copies a high-speed copier can produce in a given number of seconds.

18. Tell how to find the number of copies run in 12 seconds.

19. Tell how to find the number of copies run in 13 seconds.

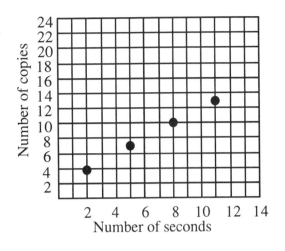

20. How do you graph the data displayed in the table at the right?

POSITIVE FACTORS OF 12

first	1	2	3	4	6	12
second	12	6	4	3	2	1

SAMPLE EWT QUESTIONS

Write the coordinates of the points graphed.

1. A
2. B
3. C
4. D
5. E
6. F
7. G
8. H
9. I
10. J
11. K
12. L

Graph the points with given coordinates.

13. P(6,1)
14. Q(-4,3)
15. R(-2,-5)
16. S(-8,0)
17. T(0,-9)
18. U(6,0)
19. V(-12,0)
20. W(-8,-3)

21. You are playing a game in which you are asked to pick a point according to a pattern. You always pick your next point by taking your last point and then decreasing the x-coordinate by 5 and increasing the y-coordinate by 4. Find the coordinates of the point you will pick on your next turn after picking the point W(4,-3).

A. (9,-7)   B. (0,2)   C. (-1,1)   D. (2,8)

22. You are playing a game in which you are asked to pick a point according to a pattern. You always pick your next point by taking your last point and multiplying the x-coordinate by 2 and multiplying the y-coordinate by 3. Find the coordinates of the point you will pick on your next turn after picking the point T.

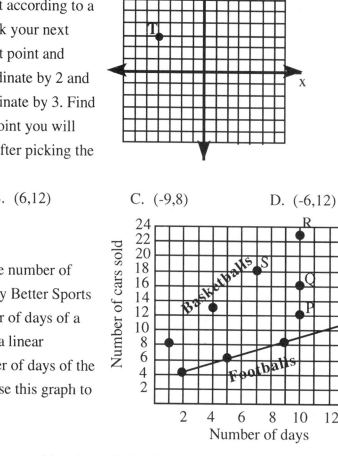

   A. (-8,9)   B. (6,12)   C. (-9,8)   D. (-6,12)

The graph at the right shows the number of footballs and basketballs sold by Better Sports Equipment over a given number of days of a special sale in March. There is a linear relationship between the number of days of the sale and the number of sales. Use this graph to answer Exercises 23–25.

23. How many basketballs were sold at the end of 4 days?

   A. 6   B. 12   C. 13   D. 14

24. Which point represents how many basketballs were sold at the end of 10 days?

   A. P   B. Q   C. R   D. S

25. How many more basketballs were sold than footballs at the end of 10 days?

   A. 9   B. 14   C. 23   D. 32

26. Consider the number 24. Some pairs of positive whole number factors of 24 are (1,24), (2,12), ..., (12,2), (24,1). Which of the graphs below most likely represents the graph of all possible pairs of positive whole number factors of 24?

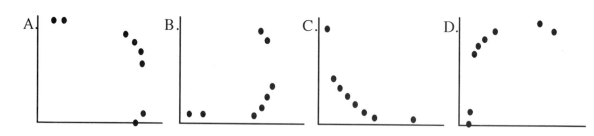

27. Which of the graphs below correctly represents the relationship indicated in the table?

Height of a Ballon Above the Ground After T Seconds

Time	0	1	2	3	4
Height	0	3	4	3	0

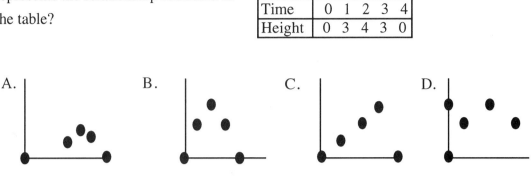

A.   B.   C.   D.

OPEN-ENDED QUESTION

28. Given: A(2,3), B(8,3), C(8,9)

Graph these points. Find the coordinates of a fourth point D such that if a four sided figure is formed, the figure will be a square.

REVIEW

1. The equation 2x - 4 = 12 represents correctly the idea expressed in which sentence?

   A. 4 more than twice a number is 12.   B. 2 less than 4 times a number is 12.

   C. 12 less than twice a number is 4.   D. 4 less than twice a number is 12.

2. Jerry has the following quiz grades: 90, 80, 70, and 60. What must he get on the next quiz to have an average of 78 for the five quizzes?

   A. 75   B. 90   C. 100   D. not possible

3. 9 is what percent of 12?

   A. $133\frac{1}{3}\%$ B . 108%   C. 75%   D. 21%

4. Objects with the same shape have equal weight. The weight of 1 box is the same as the weight of 3 cylinders. The weight of 1 cylinder is the same as the weight of 3 pyramids. Which of these actions would balance the scale?

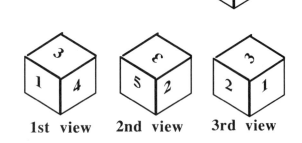

Side A

Side B

I   Remove 1 cylinder from side A.

II   Add 2 pyramids to side B.

III   Remove 1 pyramid from side B.

IV   Add 1 pyramid to side A and 1 cylinder to side B.

A. II or IV only   B. I or III only   C. II only   D. III only

5. All faces of this die are numbered with consecutive multiples of 3. If no number is repeated, what numbers appear on the hidden faces? The ones shown are 15, 24, and 9.

6. At the right are three views of a die. The digits 1-6 appear on the faces of this die. What digit is opposite 1?

1st view   2nd view   3rd view

Find the next term in each sequence.

7. 5, 15, 45, 135, ...

8. 4, 4, 8, 12, 20, 32, ...

9. A cafeteria is equipped with rectangular tables that can seat 1 person at each end and 3 people at each of the sides. How many people can be seated if 5 of these tables are placed end-to-end?

10. What group of numbers correctly completes this table?

n	$n^2 - 2$
3	7
4	
5	
6	

LESSON 18 PATTERNS AND RELATIONSHIPS
Drawing Conclusions from Graphs

In this lesson you will learn to determine from a graph whether a pattern is increasing, decreasing, or staying the same.

EXAMPLE 1

This graph shows the amount that a worker has saved after a given number of weeks. As the time increases, what happens to the savings?

MONEY SAVED OVER 60 WEEKS

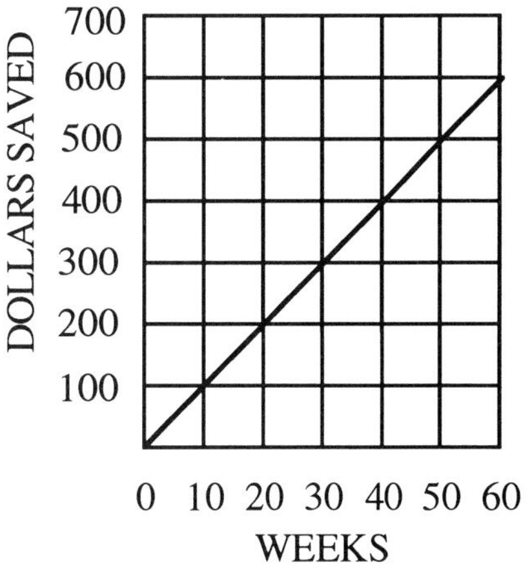

Strategy

Use sample data to draw a conclusion.

At 10 weeks the savings are $100.

At 20 weeks the savings are $200.

At 30 weeks the savings are $300.

At 50 weeks the savings are $500.

Solution

Notice from the results above that as the time increases, the savings **increase**.

$100, $200, $300, $400

increasing or getting **bigger**

Sometimes the EWT will present you with a graph with **no numbers or grid lines** shown You can still determine from such a drawing if the graph is increasing or decreasing. This is illustrated on the next page, where we will take another look at Example 1.

149

Notice in the graph below that at 20 weeks the savings are $200.

The length of the first dashed segment corresponds to $200 in savings.

The length of the second dashed segment corresponds to $400, the savings at 40 weeks. This second dashed segment is **longer** than the first. The savings **increased** as time **increased** from 20 to 40.

This graph is the same as the one at the left with two deletions. The numbers on the axes and the grid lines are not shown. The dashed segments representing savings **increase** as you move to the right along the time axis.

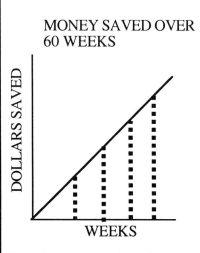

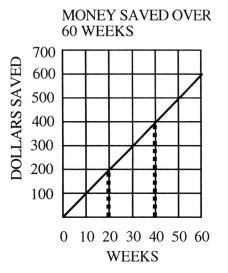

Therefore, the savings **increase** as time increases. The dashed segments are getting **longer** as you look from left to right.

The next examples show how to use the idea above to predict a pattern from a rough sketch of a graph <u>without</u> numbers or grid lines.

EXAMPLE 2   Using this graph, what happens to the temperature

(1)   from a to b?

(2)   from b to c?

(3)   from c to d?

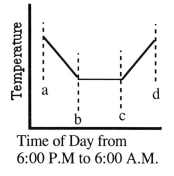

Strategy   Draw dashed segments in each region. Determine what happens to their lengths as you go from left to right. **(continued on next page)**

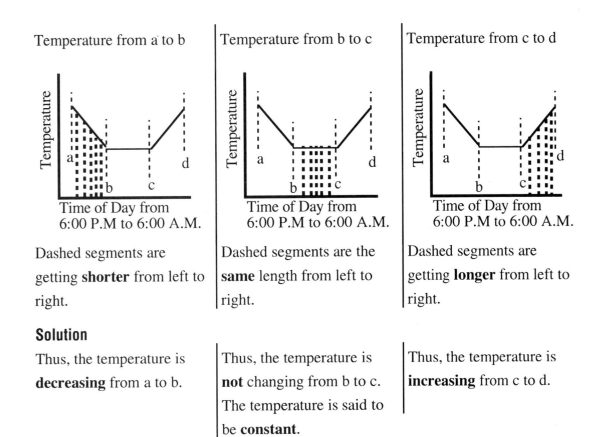

Temperature from a to b

Dashed segments are getting **shorter** from left to right.

Solution

Thus, the temperature is **decreasing** from a to b.

Temperature from b to c

Dashed segments are the **same** length from left to right.

Thus, the temperature is **not** changing from b to c. The temperature is said to be **constant**.

Temperature from c to d

Dashed segments are getting **longer** from left to right.

Thus, the temperature is **increasing** from c to d.

A line graph does not have to be straight.

The next example involves a curved line graph.

Thus, in mathematics we can also think of **curved** lines.

EXAMPLE 3　The graph at the right represents Tony's auto trip from Wall Township to Newark. Which of the following is most likely to have happened from time a to time b?

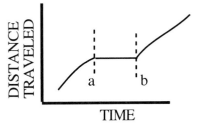

(A)　He was driving slowly.

(B)　He stopped a few times for a red traffic light.

(C)　He was driving fast on the parkway.

(D)　He stopped for lunch.

(continued on next page)

151

Strategy

From the graph, what is true about the distances traveled?
The dashed segments represent the distances traveled between times a and b.

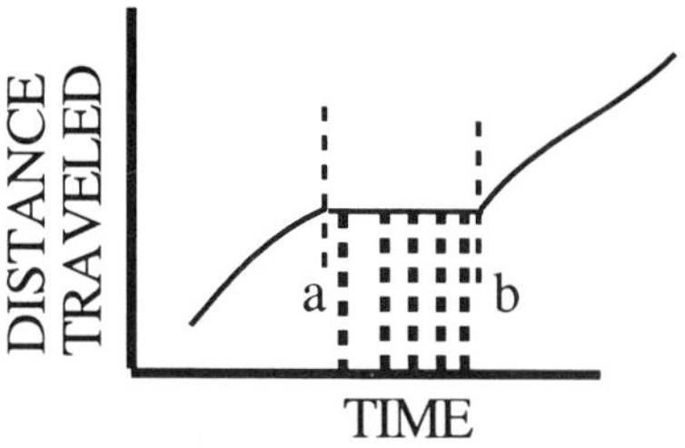

Note that these distances are **constant**. They do **not** change. If the distance traveled between time a and time b does **not** change, then Tony must **NOT** be moving.

Now let's look at the multiple-choice possibilities.
(A) and (C) indicate he was moving, his distance traveled **changing**.
Choice (B) says he stopped a few times. So, he was **moving** the rest of the time.

Now look at Choice (D).
When Tony stopped for lunch, his car was **NOT moving**.
His distance traveled was **NOT** changing.

Solution

Thus *he stopped for lunch*, choice **D**, is the correct choice.

EXAMPLE 4

This graph shows Ms. Norris's speed on the N.J. Turnpike.

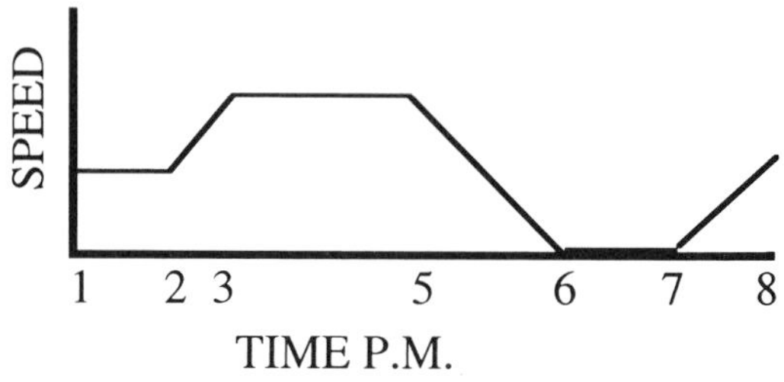

1. During which time intervals was her speed increasing?
2. During which time interval was she slowing down to prepare to stop for dinner?
3. What happened between 6 P.M. and 7 P.M.?

(continued on next page)

Strategy

1. Dashed segments are getting **longer** from 2 to 3 and again from 7 to 8.

Solution

Thus, her **speed** is **increasing** from 2 P.M. to 3 P. M. and from 7 P.M. to 8 P. M.

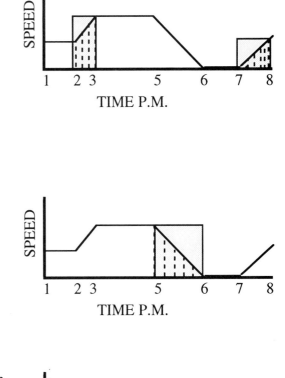

Strategy

2. Dashed segments are getting **shorter** from 5 to 6.

Solution

Thus, her **speed** is **decreasing** from 5 P.M. to 6 P.M. as she prepares to stop for dinner.

Strategy

3. Any point on the graph between 6 and 7 is on the **horizontal** axis. The y-coordinate or **speed** will be **zero** between 6 and 7. When the **speed** is **zero** the car is **NOT** moving.

Solution

Thus, between 6 P.M. and 7 P.M., she is not traveling. She has stopped for dinner.

SUMMARY

1. What relationship is shown in the graph at the right?
2. Describe how to determine whether the temperature is increasing, decreasing, or remains constant between p and q.
3. Describe how to determine whether the temperature is increasing, decreasing, or remains constant between q and r.

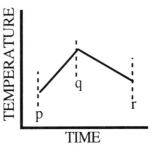

4.   Suppose a portion of a graph shows a relationship that is **constant**.
     What will this portion of the graph look like?

Tell how to draw a graph of the speed related to time
between a and b if the speed is:

5.   decreasing

6.   increasing

7.   constant

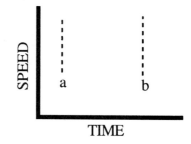

SAMPLE EWT QUESTIONS

For each graph below, indicate whether the speed is decreasing, increasing, or constant.

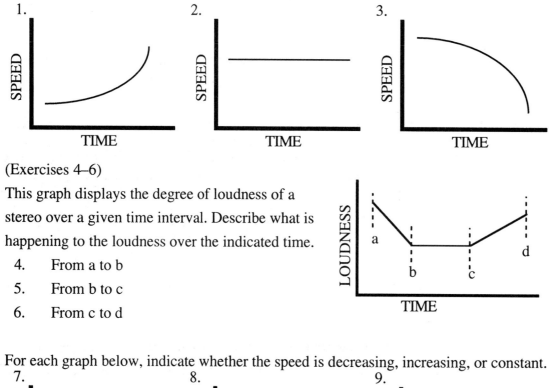

1.

2.

3.

(Exercises 4–6)

This graph displays the degree of loudness of a
stereo over a given time interval. Describe what is
happening to the loudness over the indicated time.

4.   From a to b

5.   From b to c

6.   From c to d

For each graph below, indicate whether the speed is decreasing, increasing, or constant.

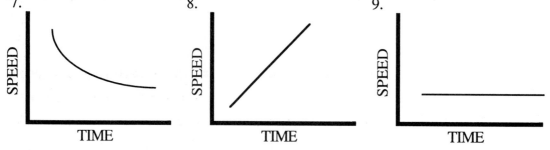

7.

8.

9.

154

10. Draw a numberless graph that shows temperature steadily decreasing at night.

11. The graph at the right represents Joan's first day of driving on a cross-country trip. Which of the following is most likely to have happened between times r and s?

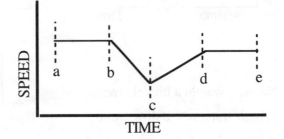

(A) Joan increased her speed.

(B) Joan stopped several times for traffic lights.

(C) Joan returned to the last motel to get something she forgot.

(D) Joan stopped for lunch.

(Questions 12-14)

This graph at the right displays the speed of a car on the turnpike for indicated time intervals. In which time interval is each of the following happening?

12. The car is on cruise control.

I from a to b   II from b to c

III from c to d   IV from d to e

A. I only   B. II and IV only   C. IV only   D. I and IV only

13. The driver is accelerating.

A. from a to b   B. from b to c   C. from c to d   D. from d to e

14. The driver is slowing down.

A. from a to b   B. from b to c   C. from c to d   D. from d to e

15. This graph represents Donna's walk from home to the Carvel store. Which of the following is most likely to have happened between time p and time q?

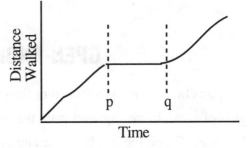

(continued on next page)

155

A. She ran to catch up with a friend.

B. She went back home to get her purse.

C. She stopped and talked with a friend.

D. She stopped several times to look in store windows.

16. When boiling water is poured into a cup, it cools off very fast at first. Then it begins to cool at a slower rate. Which graph below best represents the cooling pattern?

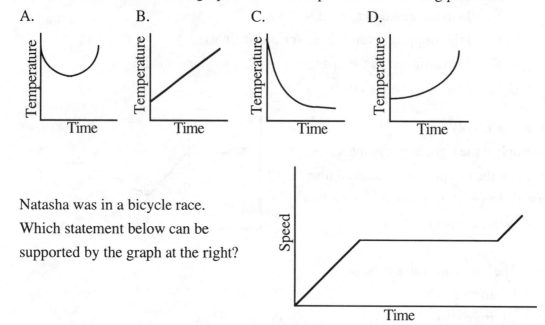

A.   B.   C.   D.

17. Natasha was in a bicycle race. Which statement below can be supported by the graph at the right?

A. Natasha began cycling slowly, increased her speed, then slowed down just before the finish.

B. Natasha began riding her bike fast, stopped for a while, and then rode fast again just before the finish.

C. Natasha increased her speed rapidly at the beginning of the race, held that speed, and then slowed down just before the finish.

D. Natasha increased her speed rapidly at the beginning of the race, held that speed, and then rode faster just before the finish.

OPEN-ENDED QUESTION

18. A large chunk of ice is attached to the roof of a moving truck. It is dislodged by a sudden gust of wind, blown upward from the roof, flies through the air, and lands on the highway. Graph the height of the chunk of ice during this period of time.

REVIEW

1. A township clerk rounds the population of a city to the nearest thousand and records it as 40,000. What is the greatest possible value for the actual population? (Use the standard procedure for rounding. If the digit in the hundreds place is 5 or more, round up. Otherwise, round down.)

    A. 40,500   B. 40,499   C. 39,999   D. 39,500

2. According to a recent census, New York City was the most densely populated city in the U.S.A. There were 4,005,290 more people living in New York City than in Los Angeles, the second most densely populated city. Los Angeles had a population density of 7,001 people per square mile. If the population of Los Angeles was 3,275,410, what was the population of New York City?

    A. 729,880   B. 3,282,411   C. 4,012,291   D. 7,280,700

3. Mr. Grigoletto ordered exactly 25 calculators for each of the 30 classrooms in the junior high school where he was principal. In response to that order, a total of 725 calculators were delivered to his school. Based on this information, which statement below is true?

    A. Too many calculators were delivered.

    B. The correct number of calculators were delivered.

    C. 25 calculators had to be sent back.

    D. Not enough calculators were delivered.

4. Which of the following is the best buy for pens?

    A. 1 dozen for $10.20   B. 2 dozen for $18.00

    C. 3 for $2.80   D. 4 for $2.80

5. Tina has a coupon to buy a skirt at half- price if she buys one at the regular $42 price. Which method could be used to find the cost of two skirts using the coupon?

    A. Divide 42 by 2, then subtract that amount from 42.

    B. Multiply 42 by 2, then subtract half that amount from 42.

    C. Multiply 42 by one-half, then subtract that amount from 42.

    D. Divide 42 by 2, then add that amount to 42.

6. Tammy ran 12 times around a three-quarter-mile track. How many miles did she run?

157

LESSON 19   DATA ANALYSIS
Bar and Circle Graphs

In earlier chapters, you have seen data displayed in data tables and in line graphs.
In this lesson you will explore the use of bar and circle graphs for displaying data.

EXAMPLE 1   According to the bar graph, how many juniors are taking Latin?

JUNIORS IN FOREIGN LANGUAGES

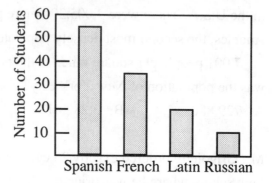

Strategy

In the **Latin box**, draw a dashed vertical.

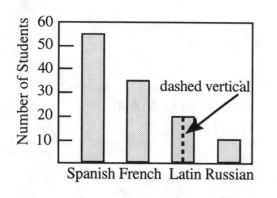

From the top of the dashed vertical, draw a dashed arrow to the left: read **20**.

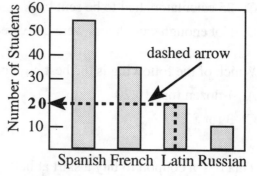

Solution   Thus, the number of juniors taking Latin is **20**.

158

EXAMPLE 2   The number of juniors taking French is what % of all junior foreign-language students? Round the answer to the nearest whole number percent.

JUNIORS IN FOREIGN LANGUAGES

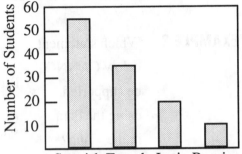

Strategy   **1.**   **Think:** French is what % of **all**? You need to add all numbers of students.

2.   Find from the table the number of students in each language.

Russian: **10**

Latin: **20**

French: about half-way between 30 and 40

$$\frac{30+40}{2} = \frac{70}{2} = 35$$

Spanish: about half-way between 50 and 60

$$\frac{50+60}{2} = \frac{110}{2} = 55$$

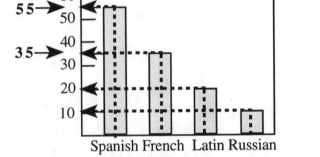

3.   So, the total number of students is **10 + 20 + 35 + 55** = 120.

4.   Now you can write an equation involving percent.

French is <u>what %</u> of all students?

35   =   x · 120

5.   **Solve.**   35   =   120x

$$\frac{35}{120} = \frac{120x}{120}$$

0.2916666   =   x

Solution   Thus, the percent is **29%**, rounded to the nearest whole number percent.

Sometimes a bar graph is displayed horizontally.
This is illustrated in the next example.

EXAMPLE 3   Which statement below CANNOT be supported using the data in the graph?

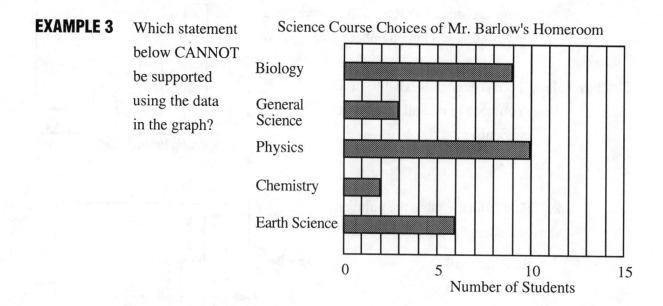

Science Course Choices of Mr. Barlow's Homeroom

A. Biology is about 4 times as popular as Chemistry.

B. General Science is half as popular as Earth Science.

C. Physics is twice as popular as Biology.

D. Physics is just about as popular as Biology.

Strategy   First determine from the graph the number of students enrolled in each course.

Earth Sci:	6
Chemistry:	2
Physics:	10
Gen. Sci. :	3
Biology:	9

Now use these figures to check out each of the multiple choice possibilities.

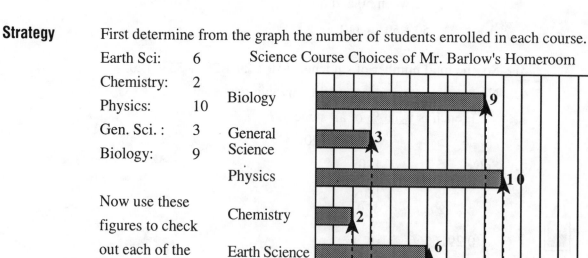

Science Course Choices of Mr. Barlow's Homeroom

160

A. Biology is about 4 times as popular as Chemistry .

9 is about 4 times 2 . **TRUE**

B. General Science is half as popular as Earth Science .

3 is half of 6 . **TRUE**

C. Physics is twice as popular as Biology .

10 is twice 9 . **FALSE**

D. Physics is just about as popular as Biology .

10 is just about 9 . **TRUE**

Solution   Therefore, Statement **C cannot** be supported by the data in the graph.

A **pictograph** is very similar to a bar graph. This is illustrated in the next example.

EXAMPLE 4   For which model of television was the number of television sets sold closest to 28,000?

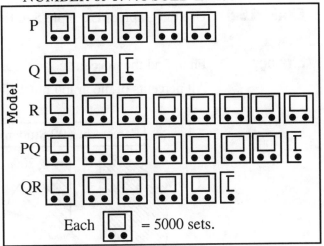

NUMBER of T.V.'s SOLD IN 1993

Each = 5000 sets.

Strategy   Find the number of each model sold. Remember, each **whole** symbol represents 5,000 sets.

Then, each **half** symbol represents $\frac{1}{2}$ of 5,000 = 2,500 sets.

Model P: $5 \cdot 5,000 = 25,000$
Model Q: $2 \cdot 5,000 + 2,500 = 10,000 + 2,500 = 12,500$
Model R: $8 \cdot 5,000 = 40,000$
Model PQ: $7 \cdot 5,000 + 2,500 = 35,000 = 2,500 = 37,500$
Model QR: $5 \cdot 5,000 + 2,500 = 25,000 + 2,500 = \mathbf{27,500}$

Solution   Sales of model QR, **27,500**, are closest to 28,000.

161

EXAMPLE 5   Find the number of students out for field hockey.

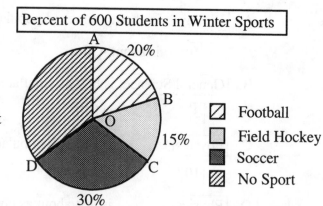

Percent of 600 Students in Winter Sports

A   20%

B

15%

D   C

30%

☑ Football
☐ Field Hockey
■ Soccer
☒ No Sport

Strategy   According to the **title** at the top of the circle graph, there are 600 students in the school.

From the graph it is seen that 15% of the students are out for field hockey. Thus 15% of **600** are out for field hockey.

To find 15% of 600, multiply:

$0.15 \cdot 600 = 90.$

Solution   Thus, 90 are out for field hockey.

EXAMPLE 6   Use the graph of Example 5 to find the number of students not out for any sport.

Strategy   First, find the **percent** <u>not</u> out for any sport.

All percents of the graph must add up to the **whole: 100%**.

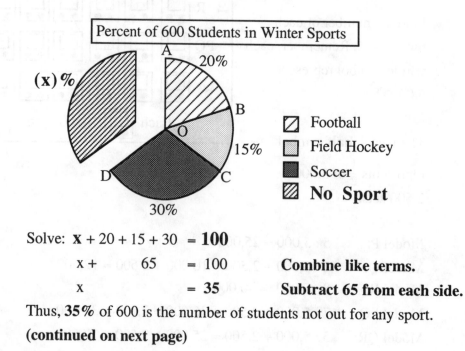

Percent of 600 Students in Winter Sports

(x) %

A   20%

B

O

15%

D   C

30%

☑ Football
☐ Field Hockey
■ Soccer
☒ **No Sport**

Solve: $x + 20 + 15 + 30 = \textbf{100}$

$x + \qquad 65 \quad = 100$ **Combine like terms.**

$x \qquad\qquad\quad = 35$ **Subtract 65 from each side.**

Thus, **35%** of 600 is the number of students not out for any sport.

(continued on next page)

162

Find **35%** of 600.

Multiply: $0.35 \cdot 600 = 210$.

Solution   Thus, 210 are not out for any sport.

SUMMARY

Use the graph below to answer Questions 1-4

1.   How do you determine the number of accidents in 1992?

2.   How do you determine in which year there were 16 accidents?

3.   How do you find what % the number of accidents in 1991 was of the number of accidents in 1992?

4.   How do you determine the total number of boating accidents for the years 1988 through 1992?

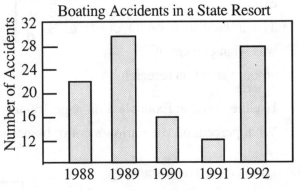

Use the graph below to answer Questions 5–8

5.   How do you find how many students altogether were in the survey?

6.   How do you find the percent taking Latin ?

7.   How do you find the number of students taking German?

8.   How do you find the number of students taking Spanish or Latin?

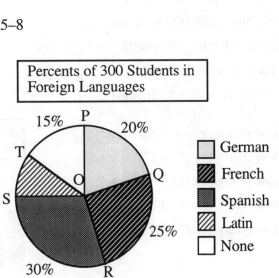

163

SAMPLE EWT QUESTIONS

1. How much money was spent on travel?

2. How much more money was spent on wages than research?

3. What was the total amount of expenses?

4. The amount spent on travel was what percent of the amount spent on research?

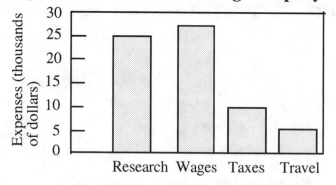

Expenses for a Manufacturing Company

5. Use the graph in Example 3 on page 160 to answer this question.
What percent of Mr. Barlow's entire homeroom is enrolled in Earth Science?

At the right is a bar graph showing sales of sports equipment.

Estimate the number of balls sold for each sport.

6. soccer   7. football

8. basketball   9. volleyball

10. Name all sports for which less than 2,000,000 were sold.

11. The number of volleyballs sold was what % of the number of soccer balls sold?

12. How many people were surveyed?

13. How many bought a Plymouth?

14. How many bought a Corvette?

15. How many bought a Chevy?

16. How many bought a Toyota or a Ford?

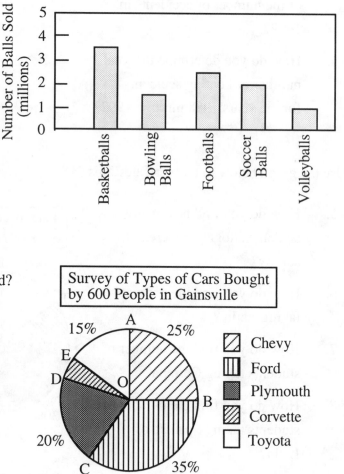

164

17.   How many watched sports?

18.   The number watching movies was what % of the total surveyed?

19.   The number watching documentaries was what % of the number watching sports?

20.   The number watching movies or documentaries was what % of the total number surveyed?

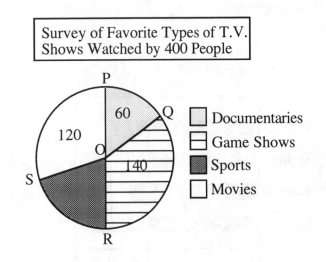

Survey of Favorite Types of T.V. Shows Watched by 400 People

Documentaries
Game Shows
Sports
Movies

NUMBER OF COMPUTERS SOLD IN 1993

21.   For which model of computers was the number sold closest to 16,000?
A. B   B. AB
C. BC   D. AC

22.   Find the total number of all brands sold.
A. 105,000   B. 99,000
C. 80,000   D. 35

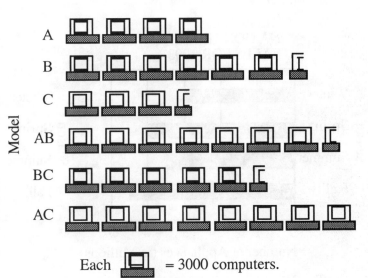

Model

Each [📺] = 3000 computers.

23.   This circle graph represents the number of boys out for four sports at Jason Junior High. What is the most likely estimate of the number out for basketball?
A. 10%   B. 30%
C. 55%   D. 90%

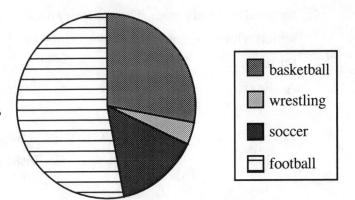

basketball
wrestling
soccer
football

HINT: The shaded region for basketball is what fractional part of the whole circle?

165

Use these graphs to answer Exercises 24-25.

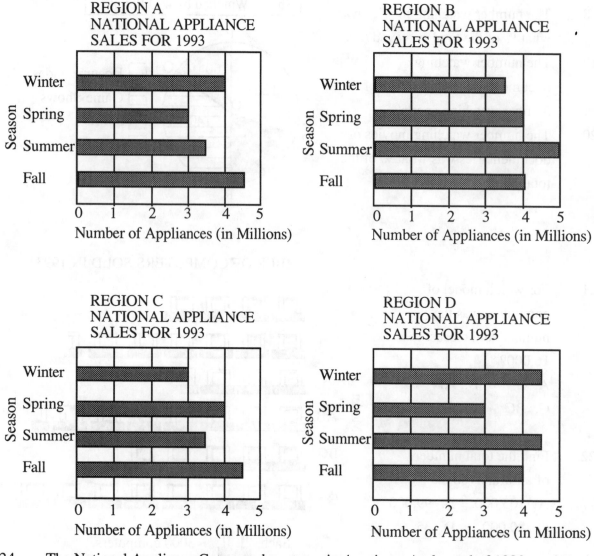

24. The National Appliance Company has stores in 4 regions. At the end of 1993, each region reported its yearly sales. The company decides to give a bonus to the manager of the region with the greatest total sales for the year. Which region had the greatest total sales for the year?

A. Region A   B. Region B   C. Region C   D. Region D

25. The spring sales for Region C were what percent of the spring sales for Region D?

A. 25%   B. 50%   C. 75%   D. 133.3%

166

26. Use the graph in Example 3 on page 160 to find what percent of the homeroom students are enrolled in General Science.

    A. 3%   B. 10%   C. 20%   D. 25%

27. About what percent of the daily limit of fat for boys does a Quarter Pounder provide?

    A. about 40%

    B. about 50%

    C. about 70%

    D. about 80%

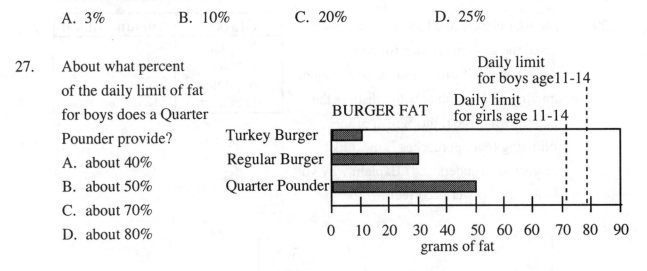

28. The number of Harrison students out for basketball is what % of the number out for basketball at Timberlane?

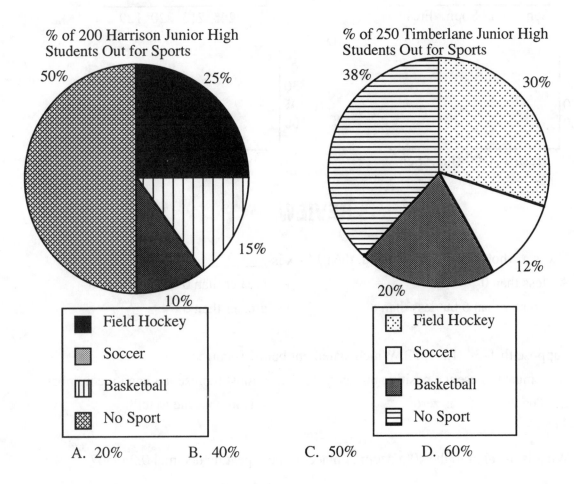

% of 200 Harrison Junior High Students Out for Sports

% of 250 Timberlane Junior High Students Out for Sports

    A. 20%   B. 40%   C. 50%   D. 60%

OPEN-ENDED QUESTION

29. The four classes of a local high school raised the amounts shown for new cheerleader uniforms. Four students began drawing a bar graph to better display the data shown at the right. Which of the following four approaches is most likely the easiest to understand? Explain why you think your answer is correct.

Class	Amount raised
Seniors	$245
Juniors	$213
Sophomores	$220
Freshmen	$129

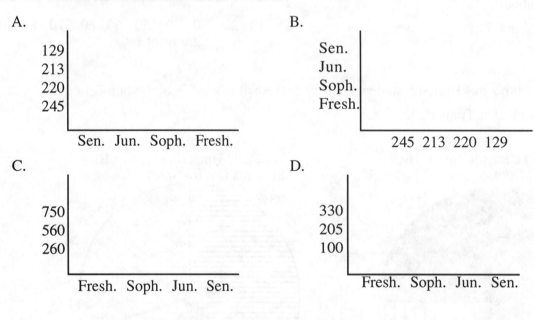

A.

129
213
220
245

Sen.   Jun.   Soph.   Fresh.

B.

Sen.
Jun.
Soph.
Fresh.

245   213   220   129

C.

750
560
260

Fresh.   Soph.   Jun.   Sen.

D.

330
205
100

Fresh.   Soph.   Jun.   Sen.

REVIEW

1. If x is a whole number less than 8, then 14 - x is _____.

   A. less than 0   B. greater than 0 but less than 6

   C. greater than 6 but less than 8   D. greater than 6

2. Suppose that -3421x = 523. Which statement below is correct?

   A. x must represent a positive number.   B. x must represent a negative number.

   C. The value of x is zero.   D. It is impossible to tell.

3. What is the digit in the 40th decimal place of the repeating decimal $0.\overline{243567}$?

LESSON 20   DATA ANALYSIS
Mean, Median, Mode, Range, Probability

A student took five math tests this marking period. His grades were as follows: 90, 20, 100, 100, and 90.

His **average** or **mean** for the marking period was therefore

$$\frac{90 + 20 + 100 + 100 + 90}{5} = \frac{400}{5} = 80.$$

He felt that the 80 did not reflect the majority of his work this marking period. His teacher agreed with him. His one low score, 20, was an exception pulling his average down. His mean was less than four of the five grades,. It was distorted by the one very low grade of 20.

For this reason, mathematicians sometimes use another method for describing a set of data.

Consider the scores above: 90, 20, 100, 100, 90.

1. Rearrange the scores in order from smallest to largest.   20, 90, 90, 100, 100.
2. What is the **middle** score?   20, 90, **90**, 100, 100

$$\downarrow$$

The **middle** score is **90**.

The **middle** number is called the **median**.

The **median** score of **90** seems to better represent the student's performance than the **mean** of **80**.

The above method works when the number of data is **odd**.

For example, 20, 90, **90**, 100, 100, has **5** terms. The middle term is **90**.

Can you guess what to do if the number of data is **even**?

For example, 7, 8, 8, 9, 10, 10, has an **even** number, **6**, of terms.

There is **no middle term!**

Example 1 on the next page illustrates how to find the median for an **even** number of data.

EXAMPLE 1   Mary had scores of 10, 9, 10, 8, 7, and 8 on her math quizzes.
What is her median score?

Strategy   **1.**   Arrange the scores in ascending order (from smallest to largest).

7, 8, 8, 9, 10, 10

There are **two middle** terms because the number of terms is **even**.

7, 8, **8, 9**, 10, 10

2.   Find the average of the **two middle** terms.

$$8 + 9, 2) = \frac{17}{2} = 8.5$$

Solution   **3.**   Thus, the median score is 8.5.

DEFINITION   **MEDIAN**

The **median** of an **odd** number of data is the **middle** item when the data are listed in numerical order.

If there is an **even** number of data, the **median** is the average of the **two middle** items.

Another measure of statistical data is the **mode**.

DEFINITION   **MODE**

The **mode** of a set of data is the item that appears most often.

There can be more than one mode.

There can also be **NO** mode if each item appears only once.

EXAMPLE 2   Peter had scores of 10, 9, 8, 7, 8, 9, 10, 8, 9, 9 on his history quizzes.
What is the mode of his scores?

Strategy   Group like scores. Determine the score that occurs most frequently.

7	8, 8, 8	9, 9, 9, 9	10, 10
once	3 times	4 times	twice

Solution   **9** is the mode because it is the score that occurs most frequently.

Sometimes there is more than one mode for a set of data.

EXAMPLE 3   Tasha had scores of 92, 98, 96, 92, 100, and 96 on her science tests.
What is the mode of her scores?

Strategy   Group like scores. Determine the score that occurs most frequently.

92, 92	96, 96	98	100
twice	twice	once	once

Because the scores 92 and 96 both occur most frequently, there are two modes.

Solution   **92** and **96** are the modes.

Sometimes there is **NO** mode for a set of data.

EXAMPLE 4   Find the mode for the following high degree temperatures for the week.
97, 91, 89, 96, 90, 93, and 94

Solution   Because each temperature occurs only once, there is **NO** mode.

Another measure of statistical data is the **range**.

DEFINITION   **RANGE**
The **range** of a set of data is the **difference** between the greatest
and **least** values of the data.

EXAMPLE 5   Moisha's bowling scores are 148, 196, 149, 194, 147, and 188.
What is the range of the scores?

Strategy   Choose the **highest** and **lowest** scores.

194   **147**

Subtract: **194 - 147 = 47**

Solution   The range is **47**.

171

Sometimes the EWT asks you to compare the mean, median, and mode for a set of data. This is illustrated in the next example.

EXAMPLE 6   This diagram shows scores received by students on Mrs. DeCussi's algebra test. The number of dots above each test score represents how many students received that score.

50 60 70 80 90 100
Test Score

Based on the diagram, which statement below is true?

A. The mode is the greatest value of all the scores.

B. The mean is the least value of all the scores.

C. Only the mode and the median are equal.

D. The mode, median, and mean are all equal.

Strategy   First find each of the three statistics:

$$\textit{Mean:} \quad \frac{50 + 50 + 60 + 70 + 70 + 70 + 80 + 90 + 90}{9} = \frac{630}{9} = \mathbf{70}$$

Mode: The score **70** occurs most frequently, 3 times. The mode is **70**.

Median: Write the scores in order from smallest to largest.

50, 50, 60, **70, 70, 70,** 80, 90, 90

The **mode** is **70**.

So, the mode, median, and mean are all equal.

Solution   The correct multiple choice answer is therefore **D**.

We now take a look at another important concept involving the analysis of data: **probability** .

When a coin is tossed, there are two **possible outcomes**, heads or tails. These are **equally likely** to occur.

Assume that you are hoping that the coin will land with the tail facing up.

Then **tails** is called the **favorable** outcome.

The **probability** of getting **tails** is **1** out of **2**, or $\frac{1}{2}$.

PROBABILITY is the chance that a particular event will occur.

EXAMPLE 7   What is the probability that the spinner will

land on a section marked S?

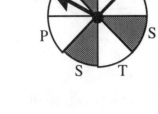

Strategy   There are 8 sections.

Three sections are marked S.

There are **3** favorable outcomes out of **8** possible outcomes.

Solution   The chance or **probability** that the spinner will stop on a section marked **S** is **3** out of **8**, or $\frac{3}{8}$.

The **probability** of an event is determined by the following formula:

$$\text{probability of an event} = \frac{\text{number of } \textbf{favorable} \text{ outcomes}}{\textbf{total} \text{ number of outcomes}}.$$

EXAMPLE 8   A bag of 15 marbles contains 3 green marbles, 6 blue ones, and the rest red. One marble is drawn at random. What is the probability that it will be red?

Strategy   There is a **total** of **15** possible outcomes.

First find the number of **red** marbles.

The number of **favorable (red)** outcomes is 15 - (3 + 6) = 15 - 9 = **6**.

Solution   Probability of **red** = $\dfrac{\text{number of } \textbf{favorable} \text{ outcomes}}{\textbf{total} \text{ number of outcomes}} = \dfrac{6}{15} = \dfrac{2}{5}$

Another important method of analyzing data is illustrated by the following.

The map on the next page shows **3** different roads leading from Crawford to Millsville and **4** different roads from Millsville to Lakeport.

How can you find the total number of ways to drive from Crawford to Lakeport?

173

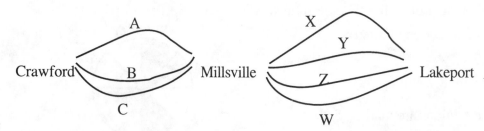

3 roads: A, B, C from
Crawford to Millsville

4 roads: X, Y, Z, W from
Millsville to Lakeport

Use a **tree diagram** to display the possible choices.

First, there are **3** ways to get from Crawford to Millsville: roads A, B, or C.

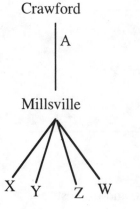

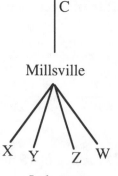

Choose Road A to Millsville.
4 roads to Lakeport

Choose Road B to Millsville.
4 roads to Lakeport

Choose Road C to Millsville.
4 roads to Lakeport

So there are a total of **12** ways to drive from Crawford to Millsville to Lakeport.

Look at the pattern.

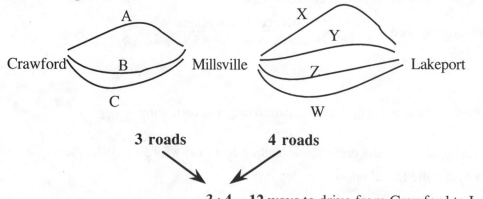

3 roads   **4 roads**

3 · 4 = 12 ways to drive from Crawford to Lakeport

174

The results of the previous page suggest the following principle.

Fundamental Counting Principle

If one event can occur in **m** ways and a second event can occur in **n** ways, then the **total** number of ways **both** events can occur is **m · n** ways.

EXAMPLE 9   A type of leather jacket comes in sizes small, medium, or large and only in single colors of red, black, brown, tan, or white. Based only on this information, how many different combinations of size and color of this type of leather jacket are there?

Strategy   Use the Fundamental Counting Principle.

> **3** sizes **5** colors
>
> **3** ·   **5** = **15**

Solution   Thus, there are **15 different** combinations of size and color available.

SUMMARY

Use the following data to answer Exercises 1-4:   21, 14, 16, 118, 20, 14.

Describe how to find:

1.   the mean   2.   the median   3.   the mode   4.   the range

If the pointer on the spinner is spun, how do you find the indicated probability for where the spinner might land? (Exercises 5-6)

5.   probability of landing on a 5

6.   probability of landing on a 2

7.   A bag of 15 marbles contains 5 green marbles, 3 blue ones, and the rest red. One marble is drawn at random. How do you find the probability that it will be red?

8.   What is the Fundamental Counting Principle?

9.   Create a word problem that applies the Fundamental Counting Principle.

175

SAMPLE EWT QUESTIONS

For the data 98, 100, 96, 95, 96, 90, find each of the following. (Exercises 1-3)

1. mean
   A. 96   B. 95.8   C. 95.5   D. 10

2. median
   A. 96   B. 95.6   C. 90   D. 10

3. mode
   A. 10.   B. 95.6   C. 96   D. 100

4. This diagram shows Mona's quiz scores in English. The number of dots above each score represents how many quizzes had that grade.

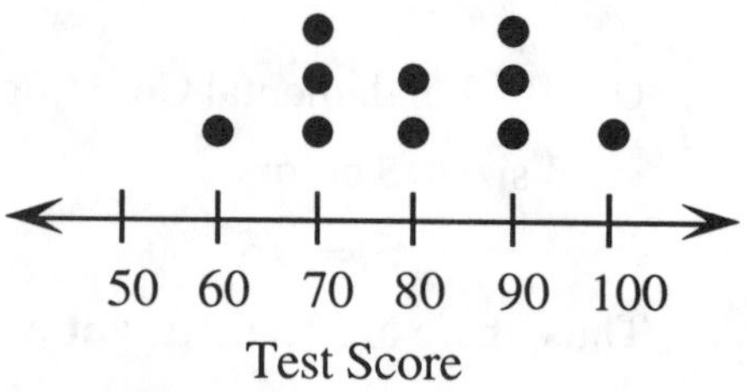

Test Score

   Based on the diagram, which statement below is true?
   A. The mode is 70.
   B. Only the median and the mean are equal.
   C. The mode, median, and mean are all equal.
   D. The range is 30.

5. Tanya's bowling scores are 200, 150, 250, 300, 150, 100, and 250.
   Which statement below is true?
   A. The mean score is 100 higher than the lowest score.
   B. The mean and the mode are the same.
   C. The mean , mode, and median are all equal.
   D. The highest score is 50 more than the mean.

6. Find the range of these scores: 96, 95, 91, 100, 86, 81, 93
   A. 19   B. 15   C. 14   D. 10

7. Find the median.   94, 91, 93, 94, 90, 88
   A. 91   B. 92   C. 93   D. 94

8.   Find the mean.   10, 12, 10, 11, 15, 17, 16

     A. 10   B. 11   C. 12   D. 13

9.   Find the mode(s) if they exist.   10, 21, 12, 10, 18, 19, 20

     A. 10   B. 12   C. 18   D. 19

What is the probability of the spinner landing on the indicated number?
(Questions 10-12)

10.   **4**
      A. $\frac{1}{10}$ B. $\frac{1}{5}$ C. $\frac{3}{10}$ D. $\frac{2}{5}$

11.   **2**
      A. $\frac{1}{10}$ B. $\frac{1}{5}$ C. $\frac{3}{10}$ D. $\frac{2}{5}$

12.   **5**
      A. $\frac{2}{5}$ B. $\frac{3}{10}$ C. $\frac{1}{5}$ D. $\frac{1}{10}$

13.   The P.T.A. plans to sell sodas at a school play. Each soda costs the P.T.A $0.35 and is sold for $1.05. The P.T.A predicted that the probability of a playgoer buying a soda would be one-third. Suppose 175 people bought tickets. Based on that probability, about how much profit can the P.T.A. expect? Which answer below is closest?

      A. $20   B. $40   C. $60   D. $120

14.   A bag of 15 marbles contains 8 green marbles, 4 blue ones, and the rest red. One marble is drawn at random. What is the probability that it will be red?

15.   A bag contains 25 coins. There are 5 quarters, 6 dimes, 4 nickels, and the rest pennies. One coin is drawn at random. Find the probability that it will be a penny.

16.   Vanessa tosses a nickel in the air 100 times. What is the probability that it will land heads up on the 30th toss?

177

A die has dots on each of its six sides corresponding to the numbers 1 through 6. In one throw of the die, what is the probability that number of dots on the upper face will be

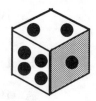

17.   4   18.   an even number   19.   less than 5

20.   There are 6 roads from Crayville to Plotstown and 4 roads from Plotstown to Mercer. How many ways can you travel from Crayville to Mercer?

21.   A sporting goods store sells T-shirts in 3 sizes, 2 colors, and 5 designs. How many different T-shirts can the store sell?

22.   Eight girls and 12 boys wrote their names on separate index cards. No two students had the same name. The cards were placed in a bag and then thoroughly mixed. If one of the eight girls picks a card from the bag without looking, find the probability that she will pick the card with her own name on it.

23.   This table shows test scores for 4 different students. Whose score is closest to the mean score of these scores?

Student	Score
Bill	78
Wanda	84
Connie	80
Laura	81

24.   A number is chosen at random from the first 21 counting numbers (1, 2, 3, ..., 21). Find the probability that the number will be a prime number.

25.   Tom's test score of 50 was the lowest in his class. Salina's score on that test was the highest in that class. According to their teacher, the average score on that test for the class was 84 and the range was 45. What was Salina's score on that test?

OPEN-ENDED QUESTION

26.   Leroy's test grades in math this marking period were 90, 20, 100, 80, and 90. Which statistical measure appears to more fairly represent his achievement: mean or median? Explain why you think your conclusion is correct.

REVIEW

1. The graph at the right shows Jane and Bill's salaries. How much more does Jane make for 30 hours work than Bill makes for the same amount of time?

    A. $150   B. $300

    C. $450   D. $500

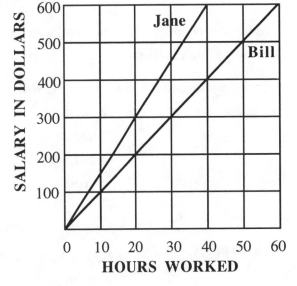

2. Which equation below is satisfied by the pairs of numbers in the table at the right?

x	0	2	4	8	10
y	6	10	14	22	26

    A. $y = x + 6$ B. $y = 6 - x$

    C. $y = 2x - 6$ D. $y = 2x + 6$

3. A palindrome is a word, phrase, verse, number, or sentence that reads the same forward or backward. The year 1991 is a palindrome year. Find the very next year after 1991 that will be a palindrome year.

4. Juanita's bowling average for 5 games was 125. She bowled 143 on the next game. What was her bowling average for the 6 games?

5. A set of numbers is such that multiplying any number of the set by 3 produces the next number of the set. The fifth number of the set is 162. Find the first number of the set.

179

LESSON 21   MEASUREMENT AND GEOMETRY
Ratio and Proportion

In Lesson 14, page 116, you were introduced to the idea of **ratio.** You saw that ratio is used to compare two numbers.

If two numbers are in the ratio 2 : 1, you can say that one number is twice the other.

The numbers could be	2 and 1 or	2 is **twice** 1.
	4 and 2 or	4 is **twice** 2.
	14 and 7 or.	14 is **twice** 7.
in general,	**2x and x**	2x is **twice** x.

EXAMPLE 1   Julie's salary is 4 times Liz's salary. Together they earn $320.
Find the salary of each girl.

Strategy   What are the two quantities that are compared and must be represented?
The first sentence makes the comparison:

Julie's salary is 4 times **Liz's** salary.

You need **representations** for **Julie's** salary and **Liz's** salary.

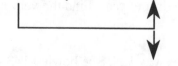

Julie's salary is 4 times **Liz's** salary.

1.

Let **x = Liz's salary.**

Then **4x** = Julie's salary. **Julie's is 4 times Liz's.**

2.   Use the second sentence to write an equation.
Together Julie and Liz earn $320.

x + 4x =   320   **Liz's salary plus Julie's salary is $320.**
(*Together* tells you to ADD.)

(continued on the next page)

3. Solve the equation.

$$1x + 4x = 320 \qquad \mathbf{x = 1x}$$
$$5x = 320 \qquad \mathbf{\text{Combine like terms.}}$$
$$x = 64 \qquad \mathbf{\text{Divide each side by 5: } \frac{320}{5} = 64.}$$

4. Use the representations to find the salary of each.

Liz's salary: $\mathbf{x = 64}$

Julie's salary: $\mathbf{4x}$

$\mathbf{4 \cdot 64}$ **Substitute 64 for x.**

$\mathbf{256}$

Solution Thus, the two salaries are: Liz's = $64

Julie's = $256

Check: $256 is 4 times $64 **and** $64 + $256 = $320

Note that if a proportion is true, you can **cross multiply** to get an equation with no fractions.

$$\frac{4}{6} = \frac{2}{3}$$
$$4 \cdot 3 = 6 \cdot 2$$
$$12 = 12 \ \mathbf{TRUE!}$$

Property of Proportion

In a proportion, $\dfrac{a}{b} = \dfrac{c}{d}$

$$a \cdot d = b \cdot c$$

EXAMPLE 2 Solve $\dfrac{x}{5} = \dfrac{3}{7}$.

Strategy
$$7 \cdot x = 5 \cdot 3 \qquad \mathbf{\text{Cross multiply.}}$$
$$7x = 15$$

Solution
$$x = \frac{15}{7}, \text{ or } 2\frac{1}{7} \qquad \mathbf{\text{Divide each side by 7.}}$$

181

EXAMPLE 3   If 1 out of 5 people buy Elley Fant brand peanuts, how many people can be expected to buy this brand of peanuts in a city of 35,000 people?

Strategy   Let E = the number of people buying Elley Fant peanuts.

Write the **ratio** $\dfrac{\text{Elley Fant buyers}}{\text{total population}}$ two ways. Set the two ratios equal.

1 out of 5	=	How many out of 35000
1 out of 5	=	E out of 35000
$\dfrac{1}{5}$	=	$\dfrac{E}{35000}$
$1 \cdot 35000$ =	$5 \cdot E$	**Cross multiply.**
35000 =	5E	
7000 =	E	**Divide each side by 5.**

Solution   Thus, 7,000 can be expected to buy this brand.

EXAMPLE 4   If 7 out of every 10 students at Wall High are out for sports, about how many of the 481 students of the school are out for sports?

(A)   34   (B)   340   (C)   70   (D)   700

Strategy   Let n = the number of students out for sports.

Write the ratio $\dfrac{\text{students out for sports}}{\text{total number of students}}$ two ways. Set them equal.

$\dfrac{7}{10}$	= $\dfrac{n}{481}$	**Write a proportion.**
$7 \cdot 481$	= $10 \cdot n$	**Cross multiply.**
3367	= 10n	**By calculator**
336.7	= n	

Solution   Thus the closest answer of the multiple choices is 340, **(D)**.

Proportions can be applied to practical problems than involve interpreting a road map.

For example, a scale on a road map can be used with proportions to find the distance in miles between two cities.

This is illustrated in the next example.

182

EXAMPLE 5 The scale on a map is $\frac{1}{2}$ inch = 20 miles. How far apart are two cities that are 5 inches apart on the map?

Strategy First, write $\frac{1}{2}$ inch = 20 miles as a **RATIO**.

$$\textbf{RATIO:} \quad \frac{\frac{1}{2}}{20} \quad \frac{\text{inches}}{\text{miles}} \quad \text{inches compared with miles}$$

Let x = the number of miles between the two cities.

Write a proportion that compares inches to miles.

$$\frac{\frac{1}{2}}{20} = \frac{5}{x} \qquad \frac{\textbf{inches}}{\textbf{miles}}$$

Solve the proportion.

$$\frac{1}{2}x = 100 \qquad \textbf{Cross multiply.}$$

$$2 \cdot \frac{1}{2}x = 2 \cdot 100 \qquad \textbf{Multiply each side by 2.}$$

$$1x = 200$$

Solution Thus, the two cities are 200 miles apart.

Suppose that a class has 12 boys and 12 girls. The class is said to have a **balance** of the number of boys and girls. The number of boys is the **same as** the number of girls.

The **ratio** of the number of boys to girls is 12 : 12 or **1 : 1**.
The balance of boys and girls in a class is perfect if the ratio of boys to girls is 1 : 1.

Suppose a math class has 12 boys and 6 girls. | Another class has 6 boys and 18 girls.
The ratio of boys to girls is | The ratio of boys to girls is

$$12 : 6 = \frac{12}{6} = \frac{2}{1} \text{ or } 2 : 1.$$ | $$6 : 18 = \frac{6}{18} = \frac{1}{3} \text{ or } 1 : 3.$$

The balance is poor, **not** 1 : 1. | Again the balance is poor, **not** 1 : 1.

The balance can be improved, that is, made closer to **1 : 1**. Form two new classes with the same number of boys in each class and the same number of girls in each class. This is illustrated in the next example.

EXAMPLE 6   The principal of Central Middle School wants to balance the number of boys and girls in two math classes. Ms. Brown's class consists of 12 boys and 6 girls. Mr. Murray's class consists of 6 boys and 18 girls. When the number of boys and girls in these classes are as balanced as they can be, what is the ratio of boys to girls in each class?

Strategy   First find the total number of boys and the total number of girls.

Total of number of boys: $12 + 6 = 18$

Total number of girls: $6 + 18 = 24$

Form two classes with $\dfrac{18}{2} = \mathbf{9}$ boys in each class

$\dfrac{24}{2} = \mathbf{12}$ girls in each class

Solution   The ratio of boys to girls is now $\dfrac{9}{12} = \dfrac{3}{4}$ or **3 : 4** in each class.

SUMMARY

Use the following to answer Exercises 1-3.

Larry's salary is 5 times Jerry's salary. Together they earn $600.

1. How do you write algebraic representations of the salary of each?

2. What equation can you then write to find the salary of each?

3. After solving the equation, how do you then find the salary earned by Larry?

4. How do you solve a proportion like $\dfrac{4}{5} = \dfrac{x}{10}$?

What proportion can you write to solve each of the following problems? (Exercises 5-6)

5. Two out of 5 eighth graders are involved in some sport. How many of the 250 eighth graders are involved in some sport?

6. The scale on a map is $\dfrac{1}{4}$ inch = 5 miles. How far apart are two cities that measure 4 inches apart on the map?

7. What is the ideal ratio to balance the number of girls and boys in two classes?

SAMPLE EWT QUESTIONS

1. A box of cassette tapes contained twice as many damaged tapes as undamaged tapes. There were 24 tapes in that box. How many of them were damaged?

   A. 8   B. 12   C. 16   D. 24

2. Jane has four times as many records as compact disks. If she has 20 records and disks, how many of them are records?

   A. 4   B. 5   C. 15   D. 16

Solve each proportion.

3. $\frac{7}{4} = \frac{a}{3}$

   A. $\frac{12}{7}$ B. $2\frac{1}{2}$

   C. $5\frac{1}{4}$ D. 17

4. $\frac{5}{y} = \frac{6}{7}$

   A. 29   B. $5\frac{5}{6}$

   C. $4\frac{2}{7}$ D. 2

5. If 3 out of every 10 students at Sheepshead Bay High School take a foreign language, about how many of the 965 students of the school take a language?

   A. 29   B. 322   C. 290   D. 32

6. If 7 out of every 10 high school students take a math course, about how many students in a high school with 671 students are in a math class?

   A. 470   B. 100   C. 950   D. 4,700

7. Tanya answered 20 questions correctly on a 25-question multiple-choice test. How many questions will she get right on a 75-question multiple-choice test if she gets the same ratio of questions correct on it as she did on the shorter test?

   A. 70   B. 65   C. 60   D. 56

8. In Stantonville, 2 out of 5 people belong to a union. How many union members are there if the population is 70,000?

9. If 7 out of 8 people use Crust Toothpaste, how many use this product in a city with a population of 40,000?

10.   The scale on a map is $\frac{1}{4}$ inch represents 80 miles. If the distance between two cities represented on that map is $1\frac{1}{4}$ inches, how many miles apart are the actual cities?

11.   The measured distance between two cities on a map is 3 inches. What is the driving distance between these two cities if the map scale is $1\frac{1}{2}$ inches to a mile?

12.   Mustafa answered 15 questions correctly on a 20-question multiple-choice test. How many questions will he get right on a 60-question multiple-choice test if he gets the same ratio of questions correct on it as he did on the shorter test?

13.   Six oranges cost $.99. How much do ten oranges cost?

14.   Three cans of vegetables cost $.96. Find the cost of 9 cans.

15.   A truck uses 8 liters of gasoline to go 120 km. How much gasoline will the truck use to go 300 km?

16.   The scale on a map is $\frac{1}{2}$ inch = 10 miles. How far apart are two cities that are measured to be 5 inches apart on the map?

17.   There are two important township committees. One committee has 8 Republicans and 2 Democrats. The other consists of 4 Republicans and 12 Democrats. The mayor wants to better balance the number of Democrats and Republicans on each committee. When the number of Democrats and Republicans are as balanced as they can be, what will be the ratio of Republicans to Democrats on each committee?

18.   The principal of Leonardville Junior High wants to balance the number of boys and girls in two homerooms. Mr. Jason's homeroom consists of 24 boys and 6 girls. Mrs. Judson's homeroom consists of 6 boys and 22 girls. When the number of boys and girls in these homerooms are as balanced as they can be, what is the ratio of boys to girls in each homeroom?

OPEN-ENDED QUESTION

19. John is planning a trip between two cities that measure 6 inches apart on a map with a scale of $\frac{1}{2}$ inch = 20 miles. His car averages 30 miles to a gallon. If gasoline costs $1.12 a gallon, how much should he budget for gas for the round trip?

REVIEW

1. Which graph below most likely represents the temperature of some water being heated up to boiling temperature in a teapot?

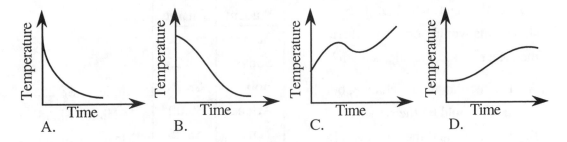

A.   B.   C.   D.

2. The Popular Jackets Company polled teenagers about a new jacket product. The graphs below show the results of the two questions the company asked teenagers in their marketing survey. Based on the data, which combination of style and color should the company produce most of, since they were preferred most by the teenagers surveyed?

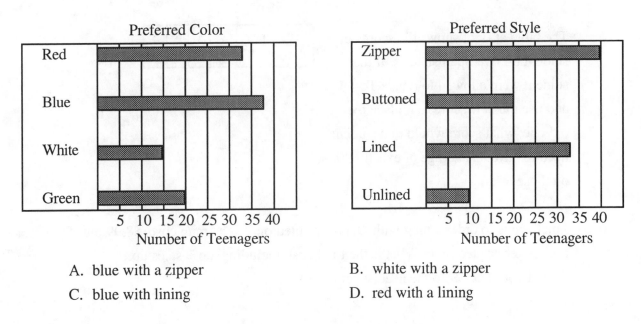

A. blue with a zipper

B. white with a zipper

C. blue with lining

D. red with a lining

3. If the pattern at the right were continued, what would be the ratio of the number of small, unshaded squares to the number of small shaded squares in the fifth figure of the pattern?

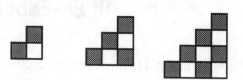

4. Jose charged $12.00 for shoveling snow. If his name were added to the table at the right, which of these statements would correctly describe the effect on the statistics shown?

A. The median would change, but the mean would be the same.

B. The mode and the mean would change, but the median would not.

C. The mode would change, but the median would be the same.

D. The median and mean would change, but the mode would not.

AMOUNT CHARGED FOR SHOVELING SNOW

Student	Charge
Jake	$9.00
Sonya	$8.25
Bob	$8.70
Arlene	$9.00
Tanya	$8.25
Fay	$8.25
Monte	$10.00
Paul	$7.75

Mode: $8.25
Median: $8.48
Mean: $8.65

5. The table at right shows the scores of a student on five Spanish tests. If that student were allowed to retake Test 4 and use the new score to replace the old one, what score would that student need to have an average of exactly 90 on those tests?

Test	1	2	3	4	5
Score	83	95	90	66	95

6. Janet wants to order a mug with "Janet" printed on it. The mug costs $8.99 plus $0.49 for each letter printed on it. What is the total cost, including a 6% sales tax? Round your answer to the nearest cent.

LESSON 22   MEASUREMENT AND GEOMETRY
Transformations, Rotation Patterns, and Symmetry

The EWT may ask you to predict the result of **rotating** a geometric figure 180° about a point. The next example provides a strategy for visualizing such a rotation.

EXAMPLE 1   Draw the result of rotating the shaded figure 180° clockwise about the origin.

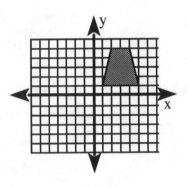

Strategy   Trace the shaded figure onto tracing paper. Hold the tracing in place with your pencil point at the origin.

Use your other hand to rotate the traced figure as shown below.

Rotate the tracing 90° clockwise.   Rotate another 90° clockwise.

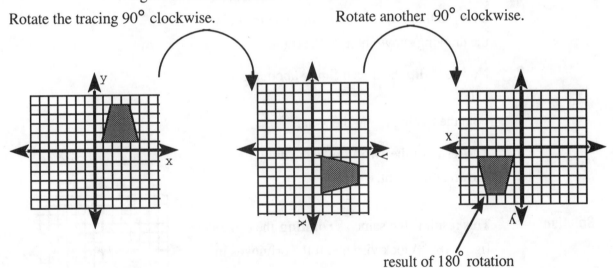

result of 180° rotation

Solution   Thus, the result of a 180° rotation clockwise about the origin is the figure shown in the third drawing.

A rotation of a geometric figure as seen in Example 1 is an example of a **geometric transformation**. The next example illustrates a second kind of geometric transformation.

EXAMPLE 2   The figure at the right is the same as that of Example 1.

Draw the result of flipping the shaded figure about the y-axis and then flipping the result about the x-axis.

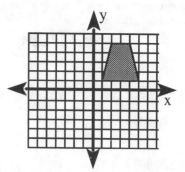

How does this result compare with that of the rotation in Example 1?

Strategy   **1.**   First **flip** the shaded figure about the y-axis. Trace the axes and the shaded figure onto tracing paper.

Holding the side of the tracing on the left side of the y-axis in place, fold the tracing along the y-axis. If it is not easy to fold this way, pick the tracing up and fold. Then put it back down so that the axes coincide. The result is the drawing shown here at the right.

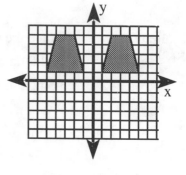

2.   Now let's **flip** the traced figure about the x-axis.

Fold the tracing along the x-axis.

3.   The result of the **two flips** is the drawing shown at the right.

Solution   This result is the same as **rotating** the original figure 180° clockwise about the origin, as in Example 1.

You have now applied two kinds of geometric transformations:

   1.   **rotation** about the origin

   2.   **flip** about an axis (also known as **reflection** in an axis).

You just saw in Examples 1 and 2 that a **flip or rotation** produced the **same** result! Is this always true?

A third type of geometric transformation is a **slide** (or **translation**).

EXAMPLE 3   Draw the image of the **translation (slide)** of the rectangle 6 units to the right. Give the coordinates of the four vertices of the new image.

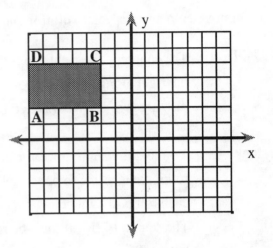

Strategy   Trace the shaded rectangle.

Slide the right edge, $\overline{BC}$, 6 units to the right.
Label the result PQRS.

A(-7, 2) slides to   P(-7 + **6**,2)
            or   P(-1,2).

B(-2, 2) slides to   Q(-2 + **6**, 2)
            or   Q(4, 2).

C(-2, 5) slides to   R(-2 + **6**, 5)
            or   R(4, 5).

D(-7, 5) slides to   S(-7 + **6**, 5)
            or   S(-1, 5).

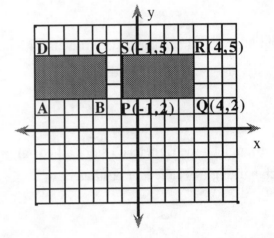

Solution   Thus the slide of ABCD 6 units to the right results in the image PQRS.

ROTATION PATTERNS

You will now learn about special **rotation** patterns.

EXAMPLE 4   The square at the right is 6 inches on each side. It is rolled to
the right along a line as shown. What minimum
distance will it have traveled before it is again upright?

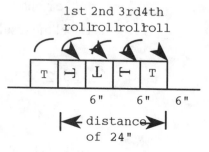

Strategy   You might want to trace the small square on a small sheet of tracing paper and
roll it along a line to better understand this problem. The square's position with
each roll is shown below.
The square (**4 sides**) must be rolled **4** times
before **T** is again in the upright position:

$$4 \cdot 6 \text{ in.} = 24 \text{ in.}$$

Solution   Thus, the square travels 24 inches before the **T**
is again upright.

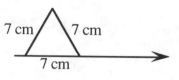

The triangle at the right has 3 sides all **equal** in length.
Such a triangle is called an **equil**ateral triangle.

EXAMPLE 5   The equilateral triangle at the right is 7 cm
on each side. It is rolled to the right along
the line. If the triangle stops so that the
letter M is in an upright position, which of
these distances could it have rolled?

A. 24 cm   B. 30 cm   C. 14 cm   D. 84 cm

Strategy   Discover this by tracing the triangle with the M on a small sheet of tracing
paper and rolling it along a line to see what actually happens.
(**continued on next page**)

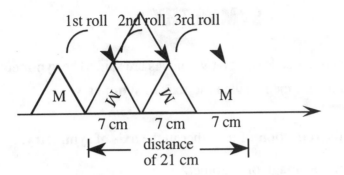

The triangle (**3** sides) must be rolled **3** times before M is first in an upright position. **3** · 7 cm = 21 cm.

The M will be in an upright position every **3** rolls, or after every **21 cm** rolled.

Now find which of the possible answers is a **multiple** of **21**.

2 · **21** = 42

3 · **21** = 63

4 · **21** = **84**   (**D**)   **84 is a multiple of 21!**

Solution   Therefore, the triangle could have rolled **84 cm** before stopping with M upright.

Another kind of rotation pattern involves rotating a geometric figure about its center.

EXAMPLE 6   If the square figure at the right is rotated about its center so that the vertex at the location labeled x ends up at the location labeled y, which of the diagrams below shows what the figure will look like then?

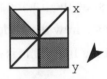

          A.   B.   C.   D.

Strategy   Trace the original figure on a small sheet of tracing paper.

Holding the sheet in place with your pencil point placed at the center, rotate the sheet 90° clockwise.

Solution   The result corresponds to figure A.

SYMMETRY

The first figure below is that of a tree leaf. The two halves are said to be **symmetric** with respect to $\overline{AB}$, the central segment, called the **axis of symmetry**.

Each leaf half is said to be the **reflection** of the other in the **axis of symmetry**.

Each half is also called a **mirror image** of the other.

Leaf	Two halves pulled apart	Flip left half over horizontally.	If the flipped half is slid to the right, it will cover exactly the right half.

figure (a)   figure (b)   figure (c)   figure (d)

You can see the results of the actual flip yourself by using tracing paper.

Trace on tracing paper the left half in Figure (b). Turn the tracing over.

It will look like the left half of Figure (c).

Now slide the tracing to perfectly cover the second half of Figure (c).

You can draw the **reflection** of a geometric figure in a line by drawing the **flip** of the figure about the line. This is shown in the next example.

EXAMPLE 7   Draw the flip of the figure with respect to the axis $\overline{AB}$.

Strategy   Trace the drawing on a sheet of tracing paper. Holding the tracing in place, fold the traced drawing over on the axis of symmetry, $\overline{AB}$.

(continued on next page)

You will be able to see the flip through the paper. Trace it again in this position to see it better.

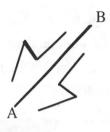

Solution   Now you can see both the original as well as the **FLIP** as shown at the right.

The **FLIP** of a figure with respect to an axis is also called a **REFLECTION** of a figure in an axis. When you look in a mirror you are seeing a **REFLECTION** or **MIRROR IMAGE** of yourself.

The resulting figure of Example 7 can be referred to in three ways:

1. the **flip** of a figure about an axis
2. the **mirror image** of a figure with respect to an axis
3. the **reflection** of a figure in a line or axis

SUMMARY

1. What three kinds of geometric transformations are discussed in this lesson?
2. Another name for **slide** is _____?
3. A **flip** of a geometric figure about an axis is also called a _____ or a _____?

Describe how to use tracing paper to visualize each of the following:

4. rotation of a geometric figure 180° clockwise
5. reflection of a geometric figure in the y-axis
6. slide of a geometric figure 4 units up

7. The pentagon is 7 in. on each side. If it is rolled to the right along a line, how do you find the distance the pentagon rolls before the **F** again appears in an upright position?

8. Tell how to solve the following problem.
   The equilateral triangle is 4 cm on each side. It is rolled to the right along a line. Which of these distances could it have rolled so that the B will again be in an upright position?

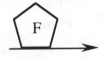

   A. 8 cm   B. 16 cm   C. 48 cm   D. 80 cm

9. This square is rotated about its center so that the vertex P ends up at the location labeled Q. How can you determine which diagram below the figure will then look like?

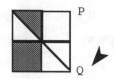

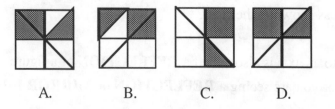

A.   B.   C.   D.

SAMPLE EWT QUESTIONS

Draw the result of each transformation or combination of transformations for the figures below. (Exercises 1-10)

1. Reflect the figure in the y-axis.

2. Reflect the figure in the x-axis.

3. Rotate the figure 180° about the origin.

4. Translate the figure 6 units down.
   Give the coordinates of each vertex of the image.

5. Translate the figure 8 units to the right and then reflect the result in the x-axis.
   Give the coordinates of each vertex of the image.

6. The transformation of Exercise 5 produces the same image as what other transformation in Exercises 1-4?

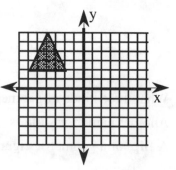

7. Reflect the figure in the y-axis and then reflect the result in the x-axis.

8. Rotate the figure 180° about the origin.

9. Reflect the figure in the x-axis and then translate the result 8 units to the right.

10. Which transformations of Exercises 7-9 produce the same result?

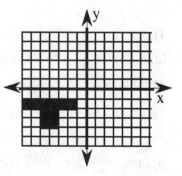

-196-

For each figure below, what minimum distance will it have rolled to the right along a line when the letter is again upright?

11. 4 in. on a side

12. 5 cm on a side

13. 6 ft on a side

14. If this figure, 3 in. on a side, is rolled to the right along a line, which distance could it have rolled for the J to again be in an upright position?

A. 6 in.   B. 12 in.   C. 36 in.   D. 39 in.

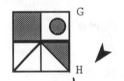

15. If the figure, 6 ft on a side, is rolled to the right along a line, which distance could it have rolled for the U to again be in an upright position?

A. 30 ft   B. 48 ft   C. 54 ft   D. 78 ft

16. This square is rotated about its center so that the vertex G ends up at the location labeled H. Which diagram below shows what the figure will then look like?

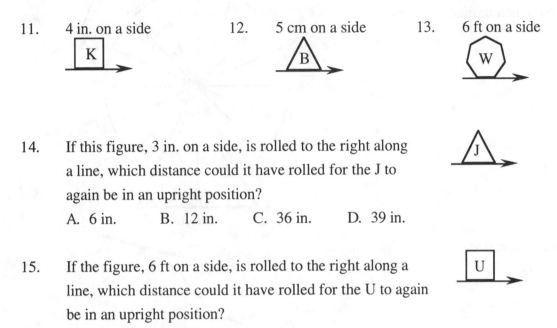

A.   B.   C.   D.

17. This square is rotated clockwise about its center so that the vertex K ends up at the location labeled T. Which diagram below shows what the figure will then look like?

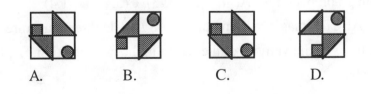

A.   B.   C.   D.

18.   If the wheel pictured at the right
       is rotated 90° clockwise, which letter
       would then be on the bottom?

       A. B
       B. E
       C. G
       D. M

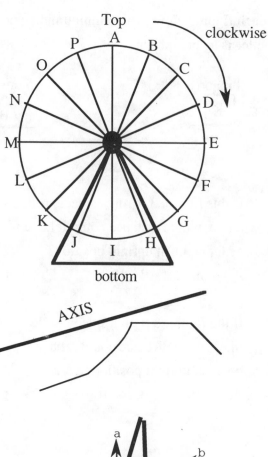

19.   Draw the reflection of this figure in the
       axis shown.

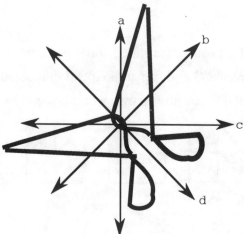

20.   Which line at the right appears to be
       a line of symmetry of the figure
       drawn?

       A. a
       B. b
       C. c
       D. d

OPEN-ENDED QUESTION

21.   Plot the following points on graph paper: A(-4,-3), B(5,-3), C(5,4), D(-1,4).
       Draw the four sided figure ABCD. Imagine sliding the figure ABCD three units directly
       to the right. List the coordinates of the vertices of the figure in the new position. Explain
       how you got those coordinates.

REVIEW

1. Thirteenth-century mathematician Leonardo Fibonacci studied a sequence of numbers like the first one shown below. This sequence was named the Fibonacci sequence in his honor.

    1, 1, 2, 3, 5, 8, 13, 21, ...

    If the sequence shown below follows the same pattern as the Fibonacci sequence, what number belongs in the blank?

    5, 5, 10, 15, 25, __, ...

    A. 30　　　　B. 35　　　　C. 40　　　　D. 50

2. Each box at the right contains only one red ball. The exact number of balls in each box is indicated below it.. The contents of each box are thoroughly mixed. Without looking, you pick a ball from one of the boxes. Which box should you pick from to have the best chance of picking a red ball?

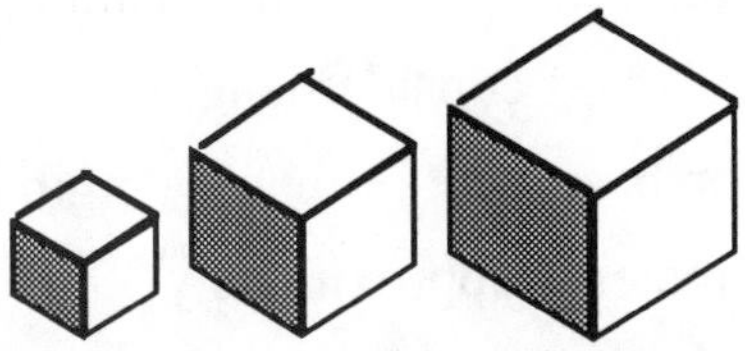

    50 balls　100 balls　200 balls

    A. the box with 50 balls

    B. the box with 100 balls

    C. the box with 200 balls

    D. It makes no difference which box you choose.

3. Which of these decimals is closest to the product of 0.55 and 0.0017

    A. 0.01　　　　B. 0.001　　　　C. 0.0001　　　　D. 0.00001

4. Which of the following is a way to find $\frac{4}{5}$ of a number?

    A. Multiply the number by $\frac{5}{4}$.

    B. Multiply the number by 4, then divide the result by 5.

    C. Divide the number by 4, then multiply the result by 5.

    D. Divide the number by 4, then divide the result by 5.

5. A box of canned goods contained twice as many tomato soup cans as chicken noodle cans. There were exactly 24 cans in that box. How many of them were tomato soup cans?

LESSON 23 MEASUREMENT AND GEOMETRY
Appropriate Units of Measure Applied to Perimeter, Area, Volume

When finding perimeters, areas, or volumes it is necessary to decide what unit of measure is most practical.

For example, it is not practical to talk about the distance between two cities in terms of feet. Miles would be a more convenient unit of measure.

But, on a road map drawn to scale, inches might be appropriate.

You need to know the meaning of metric measurements in terms of real life situations. Let's first consider length.

The basic unit of metric length is the **meter**.

1 meter is approximately 39.37 inches, or a little more than **1 yard**.

1 yard

1 meter

The abbreviation for meter is **m**.

Use meters to measure the length of a room.

Other metric measures of length are as follows.

1 **kilo**meter   (1 km)   =   1000 meters   (1000 m)   Use to measure **distance** between **cities**.

                                                      large distance   (**kilo** indicates **large**)

1 **centi**meter   (1 cm)   = $\frac{1}{100}$ meter   Use to measure length of a paper clip.

                         1 cm is a little less than $\frac{1}{2}$ inch   **small** distances

1 **milli**meter   (1 mm)   = $\frac{1}{1000}$ meter   Use to measure size of head of a pin.

                                                     (**milli** indicates **very small**)

EXAMPLE 1   What unit of measurement would be most appropriate to measure each of the following?

			Solution	
A.	length of a felt tip pen		centimeter	(cm)
B.	thickness of a sheet of paper		millimeter	(mm)
C.	length of a soccer field		kilometer	(km)
D.	length of a living room		meter	(m)

-200-

Two other units of metric measurement are **gram** for **weight** and **liter** for **volume**.
The three metric units are summarized below.

Length

basic unit: **meter**   (m)
1 meter is a little over **1 yard**
length of a room: in meters

kilometer: (km)
distance between two cities:
in kilometers

centimeter: (cm)
length of sheet of paper: in
centimeters

millimeter   (mm)
(very tiny)
measures
thickness of sheet of paper

Weight

basic unit: **gram**   (g)
weight of paper clip: in grams

kilogram   (kg)
1 kilogram is a little over 2 pounds

milligram   (mg)
(very tiny)
e.g. measure for medicine dose: pills
         or aspirin

Volume

basic unit: **liter**   (L)
1 liter is a little over 1 quart

kiloliter   (kL)

milliliter   (mL)
(very tiny)
e.g. liquid medicine

Suppose two measurements are given in different units, such as meters and kilometers.
The next example shows how to combine such mixed measurements to get a **total**.

EXAMPLE 2   Monica ran 4 km 500 m on Tuesday and 5 km 900 m on Thursday.
                   How far did she run altogether on the two days?

Strategy   4 km + 500 m + 5 km + 900 m
                  4 km + 5 km   +   (500 m + 900 m)   **Combine like terms.**
                       9 km   +   1400 m
                       9 km   +   (**1000 m** + 400 m)
                       9 km   +   **1 km** + 400 m
                          10 km   + 400 m

Solution   Thus, Monica ran 10 km 400 m altogether.

EXAMPLE 3   In which list below are the units of measure arranged in order from smallest to largest?

   A. kilometer, meter, centimeter

   B. meter, centimeter, kilometer

   C. centimeter, meter, kilometer

   D. centimeter, kilometer, meter

Strategy   Refer to the chart at the top of page 201.

centimeters:	used to measure length of a sheet of paper	**SMALL**
meters:	used to measure length of a room	**LARGER**
kilometers:	used to measure distance between two cities	**LARGEST**

Solution   Thus, the correct choice is **C**.

PERIMETER AND AREA

We now review formulas for the perimeter and area of some basic geometric figures.

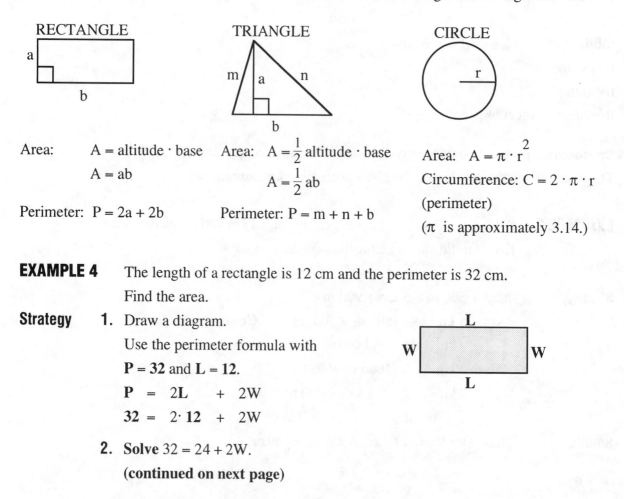

RECTANGLE

Area: A = altitude · base

A = ab

Perimeter: P = 2a + 2b

TRIANGLE

Area: $A = \frac{1}{2}$ altitude · base

$A = \frac{1}{2}$ ab

Perimeter: P = m + n + b

CIRCLE

Area: $A = \pi \cdot r^2$

Circumference: $C = 2 \cdot \pi \cdot r$

(perimeter)

(π is approximately 3.14.)

EXAMPLE 4   The length of a rectangle is 12 cm and the perimeter is 32 cm. Find the area.

Strategy   **1.** Draw a diagram.

Use the perimeter formula with

P = 32 and **L = 12**.

P = 2L   + 2W

32 = 2· 12 + 2W

2. Solve 32 = 24 + 2W.

(continued on next page)

$$32 - 24 = 24 - 24 + 2W \qquad \textbf{Subtract 24 from each side.}$$
$$8 \ = \ 0 \ + 2W$$
$$8 \ = \ 2W$$
$$\frac{8}{2} \ = \ \frac{2W}{2} \qquad \textbf{Divide each side by 2.}$$
$$\textbf{4} \ = \ W$$

3. Find the area using $L = 12$ and $W = 4$.

Use the area formula with $L = 12$ and $W = 4$.

$$A \ = \ \textbf{LW}$$
$$A \ = \ \textbf{12} \cdot \textbf{4}$$
$$A \ = \ 48$$

Solution   Thus, the area is $\textbf{48 cm}^{2}$.   **Indicate units of measurement in the answer.**

Sometimes, the area of a geometric figure can be more easily found by breaking it up into triangles and rectangles. This is illustrated in the next example.

EXAMPLE 5   Find the area of the shaded figure.

Strategy   You know how to find the area of a triangle or rectangle.
Separate the shaded figure into triangles and rectangles .

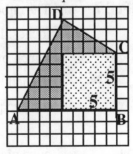

Area of triangle

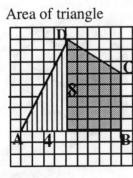

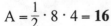

$A = \frac{1}{2} \cdot 8 \cdot 4 = \textbf{16}$

Area of triangle

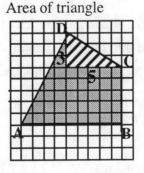

$A = \frac{1}{2} \cdot 3 \cdot 5 = \frac{1}{2} \cdot 15 = 7\frac{1}{2}$

Area of square or rectangle

$A = 5 \cdot 5 = \textbf{25}$

(continued on next page)

The area of the shaded region is the sum of the areas of the three figures:

$$16 + 7\frac{1}{2} + 25 = 48\frac{1}{2}$$

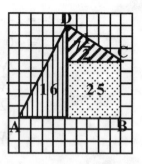

Solution   Thus, the area of the shaded region is $48\frac{1}{2}$.

EXAMPLE 6   If each side of a rectangle is doubled, is the area also doubled?

If not, how does the new area compare with the original area?

Strategy   **1.**   Draw a rectangle with any dimensions—say 3 by 5.

Then draw the rectangle with sides double those of the first rectangle.

Compare the new area with the original area.

               2.   Find the two areas.

The areas are **15** and **60**.

$60 \div 15 = 4$.

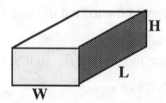

sides double those of the 3 by 5 rectangle

Solution   **3.**   Thus, the new area is **4** times the original area.   Areas: $5 \cdot 3 = \textbf{15}$ and $6 \cdot 10 = \textbf{60}$

Recall the formula for the volume of a rectangular solid: **box**.

$$V = L \cdot W \cdot H$$

EXAMPLE 7   The cube at the right is 2 inches by 2 inches by 2 inches. It is built of unit cubes which are 1 inch by 1 inch by 1 inch. How many unit cubes would be needed to build a cube that is three times the size of the one pictured at the right?

Strategy   cube pictured: dimensions   2 by 2 by 2

dimensions multiplied by 3:   6 by 6 by 6

Volume of new cube: $6 \cdot 6 \cdot 6 = \textbf{216}$

Solution   So, the new cube will would need **216** unit cubes.

The figure at the right is a **cylinder**.

r represents the length of the **radius**.

h represents the length of the **height**.

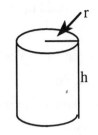

The **capacity** of a cylinder is determined by its **volume**.

The formula for the Volume of a cylinder is:

$$V = \pi \cdot r^2 \cdot h$$
$$V = \pi r^2 h.$$

EXAMPLE 8 Which container has the larger capacity? How much larger is this capacity.

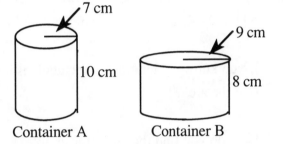

Container A   Container B

Strategy   First find the volume of each cylinder.

Volume of container A

$$V = \pi \cdot \mathbf{r}^2 \cdot h$$
$$V = \pi \cdot \mathbf{7}^2 \cdot 10$$
$$V = \pi \cdot \mathbf{7} \cdot \mathbf{7} \cdot 10$$
$$V = \pi \cdot \mathbf{49} \cdot 10$$
$$V = \quad 490\pi$$
$$V = \quad 490\pi \text{ cm}^3$$

Volume of container B

$$V = \pi \cdot \mathbf{r}^2 \cdot h$$
$$V = \pi \cdot \mathbf{9}^2 \cdot 8$$
$$V = \pi \cdot \mathbf{9} \cdot \mathbf{9} \cdot 8$$
$$V = \pi \cdot \mathbf{81} \cdot 8$$
$$V = \quad 648\pi$$
$$V = \quad 648\pi \text{ cm}^3$$

(Think: 7 cm · 7 cm · 10 cm = 7 · 7 · 10 · cm · cm · cm

$$= \quad 490 \text{ cm}^3 \text{)}$$

Thus, Container B has the larger capacity.

To find how much larger, subtract: $648\pi - 490\pi = 158\pi$

Solution   Thus, Container B has a capacity larger by $158\pi \text{ cm}^3$.

SUMMARY

1.   A meter is about how many yards?

2.   About how many pounds is a kilogram?

3.   A liter is a little over how many quarts?

What unit of measure would be most appropriate to measure each of the following? (Exercises 4-7)

4. distance between New York City and Philadelphia

5. length and width of the cover of a comic book

6. thickness of a page of a newspaper

7. weight of a football

8. How do you subtract 6 kg 120 g from 200 kg?

How do you rewrite each of the following? (Exercises 9-11)

9. 50 km 2400 m   10.   5 h 80 min   11.   5 yd 7 ft

12. If you know the length of a rectangle is 4 m and the perimeter is 24 m, how do you find the area?

13. How do you find the area of a complex region like the one pictured at the right?

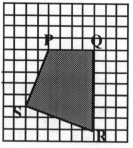

14. How do you find the effect on the area of a rectangle if each side is multiplied by 3?

15. How do you find the effect on the volume of a cube if each side is multiplied by 3?

16. How do you find the volume of a cylinder with radius 6 in and height 4 in?

SAMPLE EWT QUESTIONS

What unit of measure would be most appropriate to measure each of the following? (Exercises 1–5)

1. length and width of the cover of this workbook?

    A. cm   B. km   C. m   D. mm

2. weight of a Sunday newspaper

    A. m   B. g   C. mL   D. km

3. distance between exits on a turnpike

    A. L   B. m   C. kg   D. km

4.   amount of soda in a large bottle of ginger ale
      A. L   B. kg   C. kL   D. m

5.   the thickness of a needle
      A. km   B. m   C. cm   D. mm

6.   Kim ran 9 km 300 m on Thursday and 5 km 900 m on Saturday.
      How far did she run altogether on the two days?
      A. 15 km 200 m   B. 14 km 200 m
      C. 14 km 300 m   D. 15 km 300 m

7.   Tina weighs 60 kg 600 g. She gains 4 kg 700 g. Find her new weight.
      A. 65 kg 700 g   B. 65 kg 1300 g
      C. 64 kg 300 kg   D. 65 kg 300 kg

8.   John weighs 110 kg. He loses 3 kg 700 g. Find his new weight.
      A. 106 kg 700 g   B. 106 kg 700 g
      C. 107 kg 300 g   D. 106 kg 300 g

9.   The width of a rectangle is 8 ft. The perimeter is 40 ft. Find the area of the rectangle.

10.   The width of a rectangle is 4 cm. The perimeter is 30 cm. Find the area of the rectangle.

Use the formula for the area of a parallelogram given below to answer Exercises 11-12.

Area of Parallelogram	
A = length of **height** time length of **side** to which height is drawn. A = **h · s**	

Find the area of each parallelogram. Lengths of sides and heights are given in inches.

11.

12.

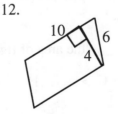

Find the area of each shaded region.

13.

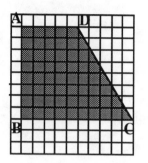

14.

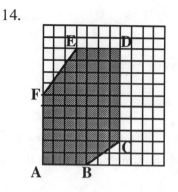

15.   A rectangle has length 8 cm and width 3 cm.
       If the sides are each tripled, is the area tripled?
       If not, how does the new area compare with the original area?

16.   If the sides of a square are each multiplied by 4, how does the new area compare with
       the original area?

The rectangular solid at the right is built of unit cubes 1 inch
by 1 inch by 1 inch. How many unit cubes will be needed to
build a rectangular solid that is:

17.   twice the size of the one at the right?
18.   three time the size of the one at the right?

19.   Which container has the larger
       capacity? How much larger is this
       capacity?

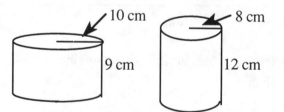

20.   Which of these choices would produce a true statement
       if written in the blank?

       The area of figure 1 _____ the area of figure 2.

       A. =   B. <   C. >   D. is $\frac{1}{2}$ of

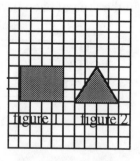

21. In which list below are the units of measurement arranged in order from **largest to smallest?**

    A. gram, milligram, kilogram   B. milligram, kilogram, gram

    C. kilogram, milligram, gram   D. kilogram, gram, milligram

22. The second figure at the right is an **equilateral** triangle. All sides have equal length. Find the length of each side of the equilateral triangle if it has the same perimeter as the rectangle.

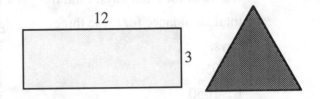

23. Find the area of the heavily shaded portion inside the triangle at the right.

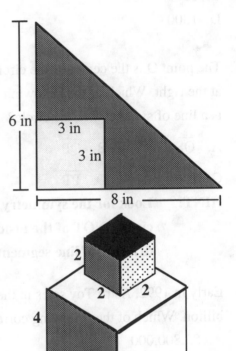

24. Find the total volume of the rectangular solids at right.
(Measurements are given in inches.)

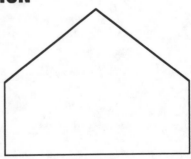

OPEN-ENDED QUESTION

25. Trace the drawing on graph paper. Measure the lengths of all the sides. Use these measurements to find the perimeter and area of the figure. Be sure to include the appropriate units for both perimeter and area. Give your answers and explain how you got them.

REVIEW

1. The West Long Branch town fair was held for three days. Find the total attendance for these three days.

   A. 950
   B. 1050
   C. 1200
   D. 1300

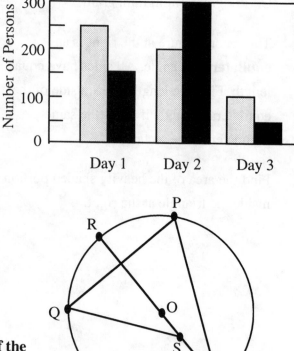

2. The point O is the center of the circle at the right. Which of the following is a line of symmetry of the circle?

   A. $\overline{QS}$ B. $\overline{QP}$

   C. $\overline{RT}$ D. $\overline{PT}$

   HINT: **Look for the symmetry of the circle, NOT of the inside drawing of line segments.**

3. Early in 1992, Astro Toy sales in the U.S.A. for that year were predicted to be $3.8 billion. Which of the following correctly represents that amount of money?

   A. $3,800,000   B. $3,800,000,000
   C. $3,800,000,000,000   D. $3,800,000,000,000,000

4. What digit is in the sixtieth decimal place of the decimal form of $\frac{4}{11}$?

LESSON 24 MEASUREMENT AND GEOMETRY
Angles, Sum of Angles of a Triangle, Parallel Lines

Special types of angles and triangles are illustrated below.

TYPES of ANGLES

acute

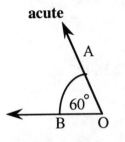

(**measure** of angle AOB)

m ∠AOB is **less** than 90

right

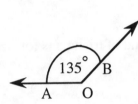

m ∠AOB **is** 90

obtuse

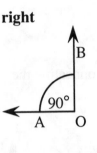

m ∠AOB is **greater** than 90.

straight

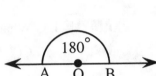

m ∠AOB is **180**.

Sides form a **line.**

TYPES of TRIANGLES

right triangle

isosceles triangle

acute triangle

obtuse triangle

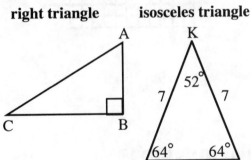

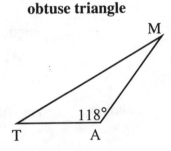

one angle of degree measure 90

two sides equal, two angles equal in measure

all angles **less** than 90 in measure

one angle greater than 90 in measure

scalene triangle: no two sides equal in length

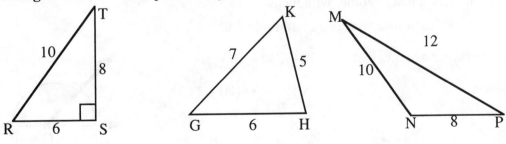

Sometimes a triangle can have more than one characteristic. For example, the triangle at the right is **obtuse:** an angle measure of 128 is greater than 90.

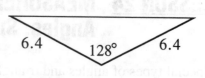

The triangle is also **isosceles** since two sides have the same length, 6.4.

Therefore the triangle is both **isosceles** and **obtuse**.

EXAMPLE 1   What kind of triangle is formed by connecting the points A(2,3), B(7,3), and C(7,8)?

Strategy   Plot the points on graph paper.
Draw Δ ABC (**triangle** ABC).

From the drawing you can see that
∠B (**angle** B) is a **right** angle.
Thus the triangle is a **right** triangle.

By counting blocks, you can find the lengths of two sides of the triangle.

AB = **5**   BC = **5**

The triangle is also **isosceles**.

Solution   Thus, the Δ is an **isosceles right** Δ.

SPECIAL ANGLE RELATIONSHIPS

Recall from the previous page that m ∠AOB is **180**.

Now in this next figure note that the **straight** angle ∠AOB is separated by $\overrightarrow{OC}$ into **two** angles:

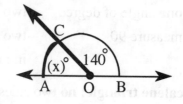

one with measure **x** and the other with measure **140**.

Their measures must **add** up to **180**.

So, you can write an equation: x + 140 = 180

Solve for x.   x   = 180 - 140

                                        x   = 40

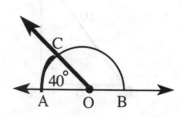

This figure shows a **right angle**.

The sides of a right angle are **perpendicular**.

$\overrightarrow{OB}$ **is perpendicular to** $\overrightarrow{OA}$

$\overrightarrow{OB}$ $\perp$ $\overrightarrow{OA}$

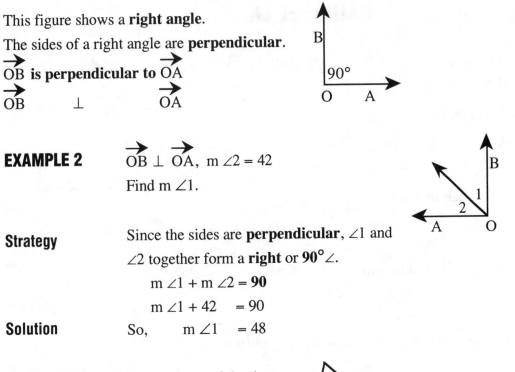

EXAMPLE 2 $\overrightarrow{OB} \perp \overrightarrow{OA}$, m $\angle 2 = 42$

Find m $\angle 1$.

Strategy   Since the sides are **perpendicular**, $\angle 1$ and $\angle 2$ together form a **right** or **90°** $\angle$.

       m $\angle 1 +$ m $\angle 2 = \mathbf{90}$

       m $\angle 1 + 42$ $= 90$

Solution   So,   m $\angle 1$ $= 48$

Recall, the **sum** of the measures of the three angles of a triangle is **180**.

     m $\angle 1 +$ m $\angle 2 +$ m $\angle 3 = 180$

The next example applies this property together with the one about straight angles studied at the bottom of the previous page.

EXAMPLE 3   m $\angle 4 = 147$, m $\angle 3 = 68$

Find m $\angle 1$.

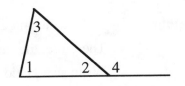

Strategy   First use: $\angle 4$ and $\angle 2$ form a straight angle to find m $\angle 2$.

Now use: m $\angle 3 = 68$, m $\angle 2 = 33$, and sum of angle measures of a triangle is 180 to find m $\angle 1$.

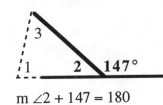

     m $\angle 2 + 147 = 180$

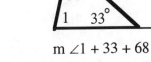

     m $\angle 1 + 33 + 68$ $= 180$

     m $\angle 1 + $ 101 $= 180$

Solution   m $\angle 2$ $= 33$ **m $\angle 1$** $= \mathbf{79}$

PARALLEL LINES

If m is parallel to n (**m ‖ n**) the measures of any pair of angles either are **equal** or **add up to 180**.

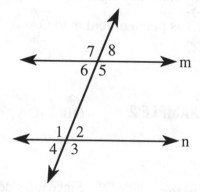

Notice any angle is either

    acute   ($\angle 6, \angle 8, \angle 2, \angle 4$) **or**

    obtuse   ($\angle 5, \angle 7, \angle 1, \angle 3$).

The measures of any pair of **acute** angles are **equal**.

    e.g.   m $\angle 8$ = m $\angle 2$ m $\angle 8$ = m $\angle 4$

The measures of any pair of **obtuse** angles are **equal**.

    e.g.   m $\angle 7$ = m $\angle 3$ m $\angle 1$ = m $\angle 5$

The **sum** of the measures of any **acute** angle and any **obtuse** angle is **180**.

    e.g.   m $\angle 1$ + m $\angle 6$ = 180   m $\angle 3$ + m $\angle 8$ = 180

EXAMPLE 4   Given: m ‖ n, m $\angle 1$ = 3x + 10, m $\angle 2$ = x + 30

              Find m $\angle 1$.

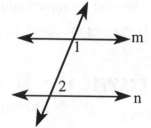

Strategy $\angle 2$ is acute and $\angle 1$ is obtuse.

            Therefore, the sum of their measures is 180.

            Write an equation.

$$m \angle 1 + m \angle 2 = 180$$

$$3x + 10 + 1x + 30 = 180$$

$$4x + 40 = 180$$

$$4x = 140$$

$$x = 35$$

        Find m $\angle 1$:   m $\angle 1$ = 3x + 10

                      m $\angle 1$ = 3 · **35** + 10

Solution   m $\angle 1$ = 105 + 10 = 115

SUMMARY

1.   The measure of an acute angle is _____.

2.   The measure of a right angle is _____.

3.   The measure of an obtuse angle is _____.

4.   The measure of a straight angle is _____.

5.   What is the sum of the measures of the angles of a triangle?

6.   If you know the measures of two angles of a triangle are 30 and 40, how can you find the measure of the third angle?

7.   If m is parallel to n, the measures of any pair of any labeled angles are either _____ or _____.

8.   Given: m ∥ n, m ∠2 = 2x, m ∠8 = 3x.
      What equation can you write to find m ∠8 ?

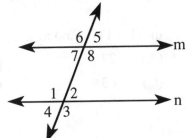

SAMPLE EWT QUESTIONS

Identify each type of triangle. There may be more than one answer.

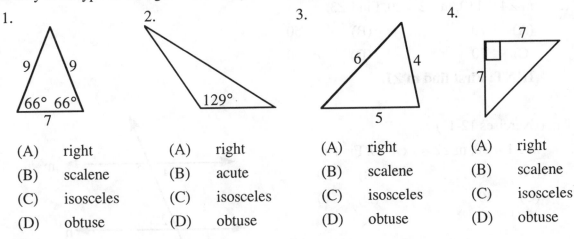

1.
(A)   right
(B)   scalene
(C)   isosceles
(D)   obtuse

2.
(A)   right
(B)   acute
(C)   isosceles
(D)   obtuse

3.
(A)   right
(B)   scalene
(C)   isosceles
(D)   obtuse

4.
(A)   right
(B)   scalene
(C)   isosceles
(D)   obtuse

What kind of triangle is formed by connecting the points P, Q, and R?

5.   P(1,3), Q(1,7), R(8,3)
      (A)   right
      (B)   obtuse
      (C)   acute
      (D)   isosceles

6.   P(3,7)). Q(8,7), R(0,2)
      (A)   right
      (B)   acute
      (C)   isosceles
      (D)   obtuse

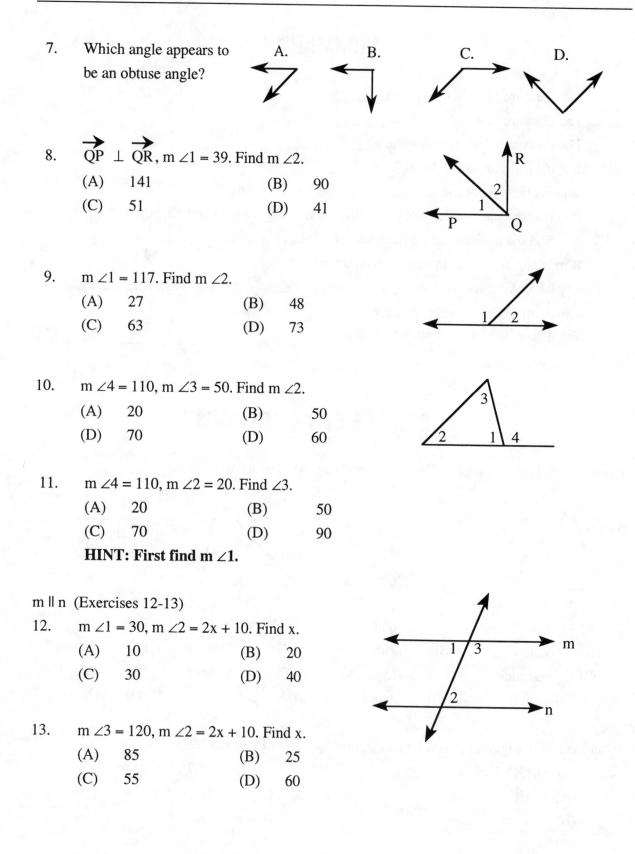

7. Which angle appears to be an obtuse angle?

A.   B.   C.   D.

8. $\overrightarrow{QP} \perp \overrightarrow{QR}$, m $\angle 1$ = 39. Find m $\angle 2$.

(A) 141   (B) 90

(C) 51   (D) 41

9. m $\angle 1$ = 117. Find m $\angle 2$.

(A) 27   (B) 48

(C) 63   (D) 73

10. m $\angle 4$ = 110, m $\angle 3$ = 50. Find m $\angle 2$.

(A) 20   (B) 50

(D) 70   (D) 60

11. m $\angle 4$ = 110, m $\angle 2$ = 20. Find $\angle 3$.

(A) 20   (B) 50

(C) 70   (D) 90

HINT: First find m $\angle 1$.

m ‖ n (Exercises 12-13)

12. m $\angle 1$ = 30, m $\angle 2$ = 2x + 10. Find x.

(A) 10   (B) 20

(C) 30   (D) 40

13. m $\angle 3$ = 120, m $\angle 2$ = 2x + 10. Find x.

(A) 85   (B) 25

(C) 55   (D) 60

14. m ∠ABD is most likely to be

    A. less than 50

    B. between 50 and 60

    C. greater than 70

    D. none of these

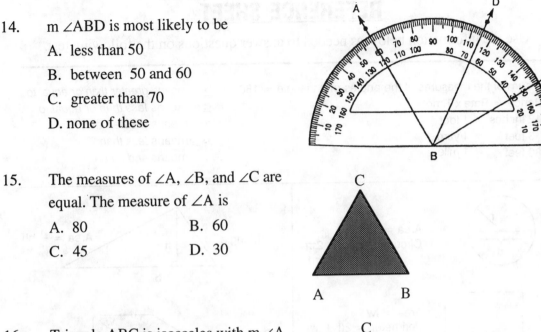

15. The measures of ∠A, ∠B, and ∠C are equal. The measure of ∠A is

    A. 80   B. 60

    C. 45   D. 30

16. Triangle ABC is isosceles with m ∠A = m ∠B. m ∠C = 70. Find m ∠B.

    A. 110   B. 70

    C 55   D. 35

OPEN-ENDED QUESTION

17. Given: m ∠1 = 70, m ∠3 = 40. Find m ∠4.

Repeat this for 4 other pairs of measures of ∠1 and ∠3 that you make up on your own.

Do you see a pattern for predicting the value of m ∠ if you are given m ∠1 and m ∠3? Explain what this pattern is. Explain why you think the pattern works.

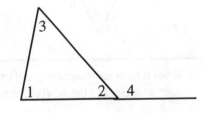

REFERENCE SHEET

Use the information below as needed to answer questions on the following test.

The sum of the measures of the angles of a triangle = 180°

Distance = Rate x Time

12 inches	= 1 foot
3 feet	= 1 yard
5280 feet	= 1 mile

$\geq$ means *greater than or equal to*

$\leq$ means *less than or equal to*

$>$ means *greater than*

$<$ means *less than*

$\ldots$ means *and so on*

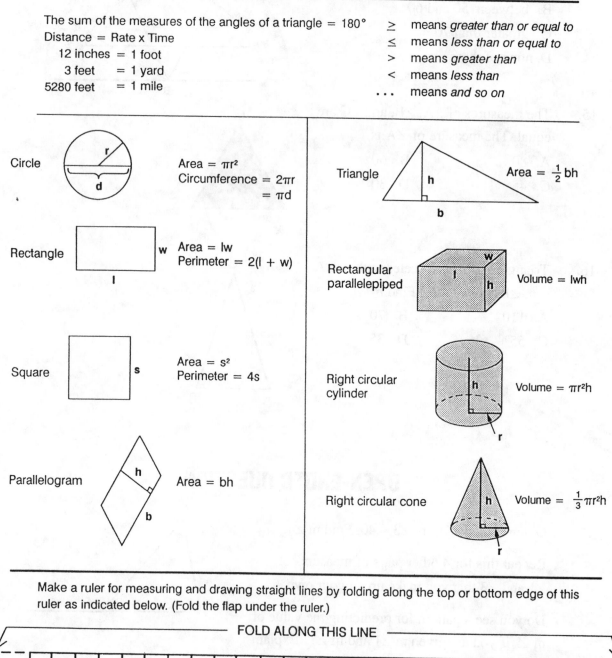

Circle
Area = πr^2
Circumference = $2\pi r$
= πd

Rectangle
Area = lw
Perimeter = 2(l + w)

Square
Area = s^2
Perimeter = 4s

Parallelogram
Area = bh

Triangle
Area = $\frac{1}{2}$ bh

Rectangular parallelepiped
Volume = lwh

Right circular cylinder
Volume = $\pi r^2 h$

Right circular cone
Volume = $\frac{1}{3} \pi r^2 h$

Make a ruler for measuring and drawing straight lines by folding along the top or bottom edge of this ruler as indicated below. (Fold the flap under the ruler.)

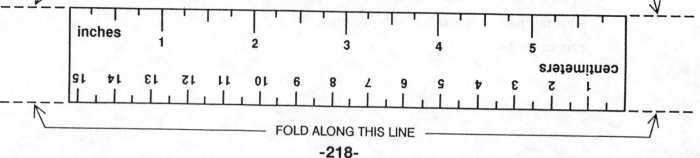

FOLD ALONG THIS LINE

FOLD ALONG THIS LINE

-218-

PRACTICE TEST
PART 1

DIRECTIONS: Work each problem.

UNLESS THE PROBLEM STATES OTHERWISE, DO NOT FIGURE SALES TAX IN YOUR ANSWERS TO PROBLEMS INVOLVING PURCHASES.

1. If the wheel pictured below is rotated 90° clockwise, which letter would then be where the M is now located?

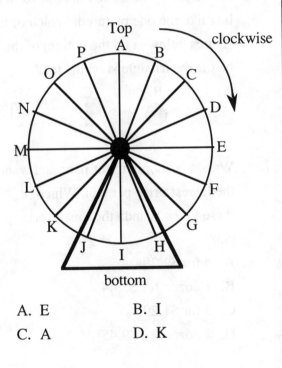

A. E   B. I

C. A   D. K

2. During a flight from New Jersey to Miami, the pilot announced that the plane was flying at an altitude of 46,000 feet. About how many miles high was the plane then flying?

A. 5 miles   B. 7 miles

C. 9 miles   D. 11 miles

3. Based on the data in the tables below, which style and color of blazer is the most preferred by teenagers in a survey?

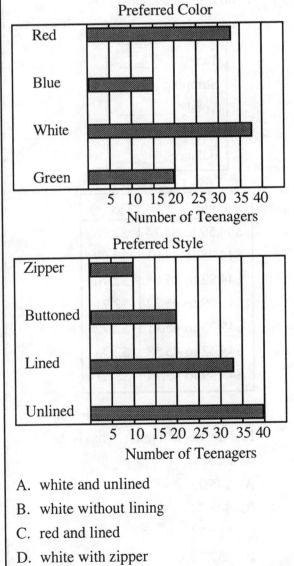

A. white and unlined

B. white without lining

C. red and lined

D. white with zipper

4. If x is a whole number between 5 and 10, then 15 - x is
   A. less than 10
   B. greater than 10
   C. greater than 5 but less than 10
   D. greater than 6 but less than 9

Directions: Use the information, chart, and tax table below to answer Question 5.

Jake works at a catalog order store. He uses the chart and a 6% tax table below to do his calculations.

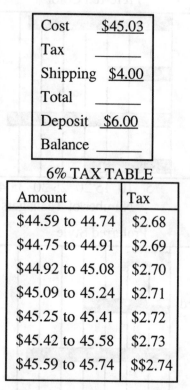

Cost	$45.03
Tax	_____
Shipping	$4.00
Total	_____
Deposit	$6.00
Balance	_____

6% TAX TABLE

Amount	Tax
$44.59 to 44.74	$2.68
$44.75 to 44.91	$2.69
$44.92 to 45.08	$2.70
$45.09 to 45.24	$2.71
$45.25 to 45.41	$2.72
$45.42 to 45.58	$2.73
$45.59 to 45.74	$$2.74

5. Using the chart and tax table above, find the tax and total. What is the balance?
   A. $45.73
   B. $45.74
   C. $51.73
   D. $57.73

Directions: Use this picture of a flat paper shape to answer Question 6.

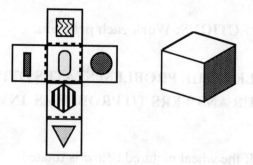

6. Suppose that the flat paper shape was folded along the dotted lines to form a box like the one pictured. Which of the figures below is on the bottom of the box if the triangle is on the top?

A.   B.   C.   D.

7. Wanda is shopping for pens and wants the lowest price per pen. Which of these gives Wanda the lowest price per pen?
   A. 4 for $1.39
   B. 1 dozen for $3.44
   C. 3 for $1.29
   D. 2 dozen for $9.45

8. Suppose that 419 = -3126x.
   Which of the following statements is correct?
   A. The value of x is zero.
   B. The value of x must be a negative number.
   C. The value of x is positive.
   D. x = -7.460620

9. What point indicated on the number line pictured below could represent the product of $-\frac{1}{4}$ and 9?

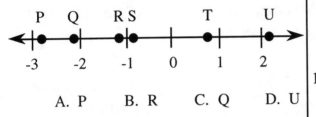

-3 -2 -1 0 1 2

A. P   B. R   C. Q   D. U

10. Mr. Jonas ordered exactly 28 calculators for each of the 40 classrooms in the junior high where he was Math Department Chairman. A total of 1125 calculators was delivered to his school. Based on this information, which of the following statements is true?

A. The correct number of calculators was delivered.

B. Too many calculators were delivered.

C. The school needed 28 more calculators.

D. Not enough calculators were delivered.

11. What is the digit in the 40th decimal place of the repeating decimal

0. $\overline{346782}$?

A. 3
B. 4
C. 7
D. 8

Directions: Use this table to answer Question 12.

RECTANGLES WITH PERIMETER 40

length	1	2	3	4	5	6	7
width	19	18	17	16	15	14	13

12. Which graph below correctly represents the relationship indicated in the table?

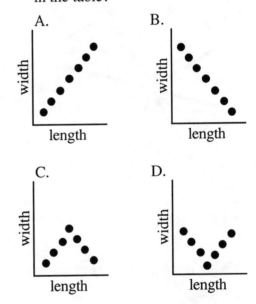

13. You are playing a game in which you are asked to pick a point according to a pattern. You always pick your next point by taking your last point and decreasing the x-coordinate by 3 and increasing the y-coordinate by 2. Find the coordinates of the point you will pick on your next turn after picking the point W(2,-3).

A. (-1,-1)   B. (5,-5)

C. (4,-6)   D. (-5,-5)

PART 2

DIRECTIONS: Work each problem.

UNLESS THE PROBLEM STATES OTHERWISE, DO NOT FIGURE SALES TAX IN YOUR ANSWERS TO PROBLEMS INVOLVING PURCHASES.

14. For the figure below, which line is an axis of symmetry?

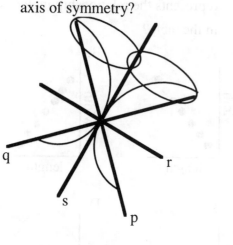

   A. p   B. q   C. r   D. s

15. What is the probability of the spinner landing on a 3?

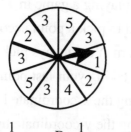

   A. $\frac{1}{5}$ B. $\frac{1}{4}$ C. $\frac{2}{5}$ D. $\frac{3}{5}$

16. If x is the same number in both equations below, what is y?

$$2x - 4 = 12$$
$$x + y = 10$$

   A. 2   B. 4   C. 6   D. 8

17. The equation $2x - 5 = 12$ represents correctly the idea in which sentence below?

   A. 5 more than twice a number is 12.

   B. 5 less than twice a number is 12.

   C. 5 times 2 less than a number is 12.

   D. 2 less than 5 times a number is 12.

18. The diagram below indicates the scores of students on an English test. The number of dots above each test score represents how many students received that score.

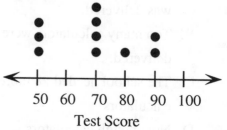

Test Score

Based on the diagram, which of these statements is true?

   A. The mode is 50.

   B. The mean and mode are the same.

   C. The median and mode are the same.

   D. The range is 50.

19. 40 is what percent of 50?

   A. 8   B. 20   C. 80   D. 125

20. The arrangements below show the first three terms of a pattern.

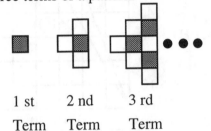

1 st
Term

2 nd
Term

3 rd
Term

How many squares would be in the arrangement representing the fifth term of this pattern?

A. 16
B. 25
C. 36
D. 41

21. Given this square:

Which of the squares below seems to have the same fractional part of its interior shaded as the one above?

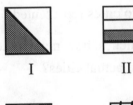

I

II

III

IV

A. I and II only
B. II and IV only
C. I and III only
D. all of them

22. Four different shapes appear below. They are labeled E, F, G, and H in the order in which they first appear at **Start**. What letters represent the two missing figures in the spiral?

A. EF
B. EE
C. HE
D. all of them

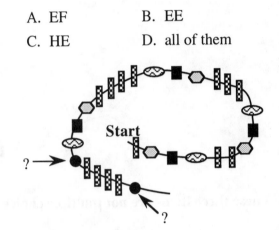

Start

? →

?

23. Performing which set of transformations on the lightly shaded triangle will **NOT** result in the lightly shaded triangle completely covering the heavily shaded triangle?

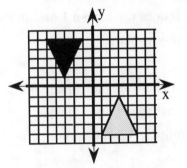

A. translation 6 units to the left followed by reflection in the x-axis
B. translation 3 units to the left followed by reflection in the x-axis
C. rotation of 180° about the origin
D. reflection in the x-axis followed by reflection in the y-axis

24. The speed of Car B, at the right, is what percent of the speed of Car A at 10 seconds?

    A. 70   B. 3

    C. 14.3   D. 50

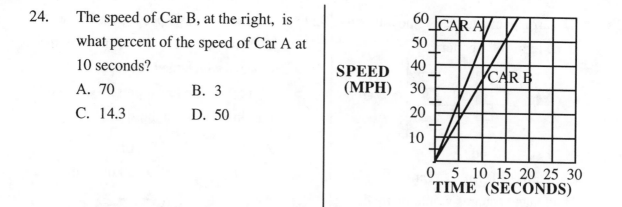

SPEED (MPH)

TIME (SECONDS)

PART 3

These three items are not multiple choice. Write your answers on a separate sheet of paper.

25. What number has all the following characteristics?

    It is greater than 40.
    It is less than 50
    It is a prime number.
    It does not have a 1 or 7 in its units (ones) place.

26. What is the area in square units of the unshaded portion inside the 11-unit-by-12-unit square?

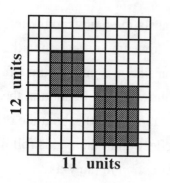

12 units

11 units

27. Solve for x:
    $64 = 4x + 24$

28. The scale on a map indicates that $\frac{1}{4}$ represents 60 miles. If the distance between two cities represented on that map is $1\frac{1}{4}$ inches, how many miles apart are the actual cities?

PART 4

DIRECTIONS: Write your answers on a separate sheet of paper. For each question, give enough explanation so that a scorer can understand your solution. You will be graded on the quality of your thinking, as reflected in your explanations, as well as the correctness of your answers.

29. Use the inches side of the ruler on the Mathematics Reference Sheet included in this section. Determine the lengths of the sides of the figure below.

Use these measurements to find the perimeter and area of the figure. Be sure to include the appropriate units of measure for both perimeter and area. Give your answers and explain how you got them.

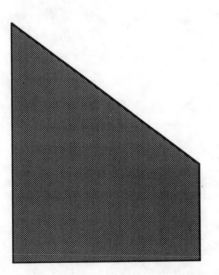

Directions: Use these diagrams to answer Question 30.

The hexagon in figure A has a perimeter of 12 units.

Figure A

Two hexagons placed side by side as in figure B below form a shape which has a perimeter 20 units.

Figure B

Three hexagons placed side by side as in figure C below form a shape which has a perimeter of 28 units.

Figure C

30. If the pattern indicated above were continued, what would be the perimeter of the shape formed by 6 of these hexagons placed side by side? Give your answer and explain how you got it.